FUNCTIONAL
TRAINING FOR ATHLETES AT ALL LEVELS

FUNCTIONAL TRAINING FOR ATHLETES AT ALL LEVELS

Workouts for Agility, Speed and Power

JAMES C. RADCLIFFE

Photography by **Andy Mogg**

Ulysses Press

Published in the United States by Ulysses Press
P.O. Box 3440
Berkeley, CA 94703
www.ulyssespress.com

ISBN10: 1-56975-584-1
ISBN13: 978-1-56975-584-6
Library of Congress Control Number 2006907933

Printed in Canada by Webcom

10 9 8 7 6 5 4 3 2 1

Editorial/Production	Lily Chou, Claire Chun, Matt Orendorff, Steven Zah Schwartz, Elyce Petker
Index	Sayre Van Young
Cover design	what!design @ whatweb.com
Interior photographs	Andy Mogg except on pages 17, 91, 99, 114–19, 136 (except variation), 150 © Jack Liu; pages 6, 21, 37 © Eric Evans
Cover photographs	*front:* Andy Mogg *back:* football and soccer players © Eric Evans; basketball players © photos.com
Models	Tim Herring, Daron Johnson, James Radcliffe, Jesus Sanchez

Distributed by Publishers Group West

Please Note
This book has been written and published strictly for informational purposes, and in no way should be used as a substitute for consultation with health care professionals. You should not consider educational material herein to be the practice of medicine or to replace consultation with a physician or other medical practitioner. The author and publisher are providing you with information in this work so that you can have the knowledge and can choose, at your own risk, to act on that knowledge. The author and publisher also urge all readers to be aware of their health status and to consult health care professionals before beginning any health program.

To the Lopezes: Mike Jr., Cath and Mike Sr.
True inspiration in training, sport and, especially, life

table of contents

part one:

overview

why train for function?

Anyone who participates in athletics and wants to enhance themselves both health- and performance-wise needs a training program that 1) prepares them for the rigors of the sport and its movements, and 2) improves the technical and physiological aspects of how the sport is performed. It's rare to find a sport or athletic activity that does not involve posture, balance, stability and mobility.

The majority of games are played upright, on the feet, and flexing, extending and rotating in various directions. Training these functions will only help to improve performance, in addition to keeping you healthier. The ability to move with mobility and stability serves to keep you on the right track to success, and *Functional Training* will show you the way.

Many therapists, trainers, coaches and practitioners are doing a great deal of remark-able work in the area of train-ing with a "functional" purpose. But what exactly is "functional training"? If you type the term in an internet search engine, thousands of sites with hundreds of differ-ent definitions will appear. Similarly, ask ten well-known, experienced practitioners how they'd define "functional train-ing" and you might get ten unique answers.

Vern Gambetta, author, clinician, track coach, and for-mer NBA and MLB strength and conditioning coach, has had a lot of practice explain-ing, defining and answering inquiries about this concept that he helped create. He states that functional training "incorporates a full spectrum of training designed to elicit the optimum adaptive response appropriate for the sport or activity being trained for." Mike Boyle, another accom-plished coach and innovative practitioner of this concept, explains that functional train-ing is purposeful training, and is represented as "sports general training." Basically, this training employs the handling of one's body weight in all planes of movement.

The intention of this book is not to encompass all of the functional training methodologies being utilized today. On the contrary, the scope of *Functional Training* is to use some of the concepts behind, as Gambetta suggests, a functional path.

Author Jim Radcliffe, right, demonstrates a move.

benefits of functional training

Within the realm of all sports exists the need for several components of true athleticism: strength, speed and agility. These three can be summed up in one simple word—*power*. As you study sport, you realize that one without the others is extremely limiting.

All athletes seek power. Much of athletic training can be derived from simple physics, with the formula for power being the main focus. As depicted in Figure 1, training "functionally" is using the formula and increasing your ability to create force by increasing strength. Strength x speed (or, as some professors would advise, force over time) is power. However, the participant who uses functional training principles will not neglect the distance aspect. The ability to produce the optimal amount of force in the least amount of time, and through the greatest distance, is athletic power.

In order to be at your most powerful, you: 1) must possess enough strength to exert optimal amounts of force versus the effects of gravity; 2) do so throughout the greatest distance allowed by the length, mobility, and coordination of your body, either pushing or pulling across the torso; and 3) do so in the least amount of time for the greatest efficiency of total work. Using these three components together, and in concert with one another, aids success in athletic performance (see Figure 1).

For athletes, strength in the form of force application is not functional unless it can be applied with an upright posture and balanced on one or both feet. Speed and agility are not functional if the body's joints are not mobile or stable enough to apply the force and/or change direction necessary for both safe and successful performance. Therefore, the *function* of athletic power is strong postural applications of force, balanced across the torso and stabilized by the

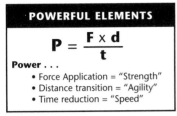

POWERFUL ELEMENTS

$$P = \frac{F \times d}{t}$$

Power . . .
- Force Application = "Strength"
- Distance transition = "Agility"
- Time reduction = "Speed"

Figure 1.

joints that cross the torso, at speeds and directions that are optimal for successful performance.

Training with the concepts presented in this book will allow you to increase the amounts of force you apply (strength development). Although many programs do this, the functional training method develops force by using techniques that coordinate the use of your entire body. For example, many runners improve their strength to help their ability to run. However, runners who don't keep a high hip posture or tall running stance (a posture we call "sitting") don't take each stride efficiently. Therefore, as they get "stronger" from their more traditional training, most of it is wasted on their inability to use this force to improve the efficiency of their strides, not to mention the injury factors that can arise from inappropriate form and technique.

Functional training will help to improve the distance (posture) throughout which the increased force production

will travel. The third component, efficient time reduction (speed development), will be another product. Using the example of the runners, once they have improved their ability to produce force through proper posture and technique, they'll improve their landings and take-offs, and the efficiency of how their limbs move about their torso, thus decreasing the amount of time and effort to do so. Many people train hard for years, never realizing true success in overall performance. Training with more of a "functional" mentality can help achieve greater success in overall performance and health.

Posture

Posture is the way we hold our bodies; in order to maintain our positioning, we constantly make subtle adjustments, called postural sway. Functional training improves the ability to maintain proper athletic postures in flexed, extended and rotated positions involving different planes of movement. It makes particularly good sense when applied to postural actions during flight (between each take-off and landing).

Take a look at any field or court sport such as soccer, football or basketball. Study

the postures of the athletes who change direction the most quickly and powerfully. You'll see them bending their knees and hips, yet their shoulders remain up and their backs are flat or arched, not rounded. If you were to take a photo of them at the exact moment of direction change or take-off, they would almost look as if they were going to jump, due to the fact that they are flexed in the power-producing parts of the body and erect in the areas above their center of gravity; they therefore exhibit complete control of where they're going.

A simpler example is to observe a sprinter. When mov-

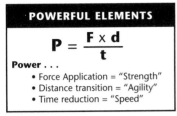

ing at very high velocities, the lower body exhibits power by keeping one leg flexed for flight and the other extended for push-off; the upper body maintains an upright (or tall) and somewhat rigid, yet relaxed, posture. This allows all of the movements to be directed in the proper direction and with the utmost efficiency. All athletic technique development is geared toward moving from a multitude of positions while using the proper posture to direct the body to the desired goals as efficiently as possible.

Balance

"Balance is simply the ability to maintain a stable and specific orientation in relation to the immediate environment" (Oxford 1998). We do it all day long, whether we're standing or moving. There are two main types of balance: static and dynamic. Functional training deals with dynamic balance, constantly working on your ability to maintain equilibrium by having you change direction rapidly while on one foot. Any sport that involves running, jumping, kicking, swinging, and/or skating (e.g., tennis, hockey, martial arts, baseball, golf) employs movements of power by shifting weight from one leg to the other. Sports that require powerful take-off and landing movements off of one leg only (football, basketball, soccer, track and field) utilize a higher degree of balance. The ability to maintain a solid and capable position over a small base of support is the key to avoiding a tackler, getting away from an opponent, getting to a ball, swinging a bat or racquet and, above all, directing your forces in the areas necessary to perform successfully.

Stability

People who are unable to stabilize their hip or knee joints, due to degeneration of the muscles, tendons and ligaments that surround those joints, often limp excessively, drag the limb, or even need canes, crutches and/or other devices to help them move. When engaging in fast changes of direction, especially the smaller movements of accuracy such as throwing, kicking, jumping, and swinging, the ability to keep joints in line with the direction of force is of utmost importance. Functional training constantly and continuously challenges a joint's ability to withstand mechanical shocks and movements without becoming displaced. The drill progressions in this book develop the types of stabilization that improve directional perform-

ance, change of direction performance, and continued health and performance— the optimal form of stability.

Landing and taking off with great force over a small base of support (such as one foot and the planted leg) while running, turning or twisting requires the stabilization of all joints, tendons and ligaments involved—this means anyone who is planting his foot to turn and change direction at high speed, or someone who is kicking or swinging or throwing an implement with high-speed force. Without stabilization, not only is performance poor, but incidence of injury is high.

Mobility

Mobility is range of motion about every joint in our body, especially the major joints that branch from the torso. Functional movement training pays constant and consistent attention to mobility, especially around the core of the body. This book, and the functional training of athletic movement, makes sure every action, from the first warm-up movement to the final drill of the session, demands attention to technically sound ranges of motion in all of the desired directions.

In his book on *Training Theory*, Frank Dick, former

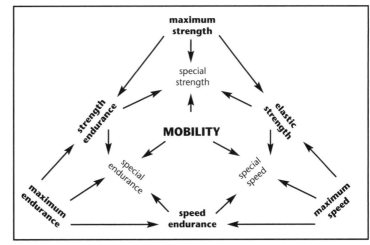

Figure 2.

director of coaching for British Athletics, gave a model on the development of basic physical characteristics (Figure 2). It places mobility, which he considered "the range through which force can be efficiently (technique) applied," right in the middle of a triangle of interacting conditioning aspects such as strength, speed and endurance. This mobility then aids the development of more specialized strength, speed and endurance training.

I have found this model very helpful and like to take it a step farther by suggesting that it's also similar to a pyramid. The Egyptian pyramids have stood the test of time, just as athletes hope to do throughout the course of their careers. The cornerstones remain the same, being increased maximal capacities of strength, speed and durability.

Just as the pyramid builders were precise in the lines and angles of their structures, we must properly blend the maximums together and then apply those to the specific or "special" needs of what can give us optimal mobility for our specific sport or endeavor. Too often athletes (and coaches) look at F. Dick's model with the arrows and try to employ everything together, not understanding the need for progressions to foster "better building blocks," so to speak.

It's understood that endurance specifics for a middle-distance runner are not the same as those for a volleyball player; the strength specifics for a swimmer are not exactly the same as those for a football lineman; the speed needs for a soccer player are different from those of a wrestler. Therefore, even though the foundations of these different pyramids may closely resemble one another, the specialized walls might not. It's from this concept that we hope to create the ultimate athletic pyramid, with the top of the pyramid being optimal mobility. Each athlete develops into the strongest, fastest, most durable—therefore the most *mobile*—performer for his/her particular endeavor.

Physical therapist Paul Chek has stated that we need to relearn the ability to move as our ancestors (most specifically cavemen) could. The ability to squat fully was needed to gather food. The ability to lunge and twist, climb and crawl, throw and carry were necessary to hunt, travel and survive. These movements have not been lost to every human in our culture today, but for a great number, including those who are attempting to be high-level athletes, these abilities are fading. We find ourselves in situations where we're constantly being persuaded to avoid movements that were once a necessary part of life. For instance, doing full squats with complete range of motion through the hips and knees, or twisting while stepping forward, are reportedly bad for the joints. There's no question we've evolved into a softer society as far as ease of movement, but athletes still need many of the same movement capabilities for performance survival. The concept of creating great force over a small base of support, and the reflexes that are necessary to do so, is premium in the development of a more mobile athlete.

A surprising number of athletes have a low percentage of athletic readiness as far as hip mobility; a stable base of support surrounding the trunk of the body (torso structuring); knowledge of movement mechanics; lean body mass; and foot, ankle, knee and hip integrity. In addition, they have a high percentage of athletic unreadiness due to a more sedentary lifestyle, poorer nutrition, improper running (especially foot/ankle) mechanics, less physical education and torso structuring (in other words, children climb less trees), and high competitive age versus infantile training age (which means they've been involved in competitive sports such as Little League baseball/softball, youth soccer, etc., but haven't been taking part in progressive physical education and movement training). In order to progress efficiently and successfully, you must be prepared to train and develop, not from scratch, but sometimes from a point behind zero training level—not to train, but often to retrain!

function of warm-up

First and foremost, the warm-up prepares the body for performance, whether it be in training, practice or competition. A great deal of current clinical and practical research reinforces the concept that dynamic preparation is far more beneficial than a series of passive and static stretches. Once we understand that athletic performance is dynamic in nature, then we understand that preparation for it must also be dynamic.

Essentially, a warm-up consists of movements that raise the core temperature of the body; there should be slight perspiration. These movements work in all planes and directions (frontal, sagittal, transverse, forward, lateral, backward), and foster the posture, balance, stability and flexibility of the athlete. A warm-up should begin gradually then progress to a tempo corresponding to the pace of practice and/or competition (from walk to skip to run).

The warm-up is the first opportunity during a workout session in which you can improve athleticism. Although it can have a "general" nature to it, it's an ideal time to utilize movements that optimize form, technique and the mobilization of the same skills needed for your sport. The majority of athletes entering the interscholastic and intercollegiate realm these days have poor hip mobility, torso structuring, movement mechanics, and foot, ankle, knee and hip integrity. The warm-up is a prime occasion to begin the development and improvement of these areas.

function of core training

Core strength work is the foundation for all other strength work—any and all powerful movements begin with the core, so therefore the training should as well. According to Tommy Kono, a world-class Olympic weightlifter, official and coach, "The seat of power comes from the powerful hip and buttock muscles. From here the power radiates outward and the muscle groups become weaker in proportion to the distance from the center of the body.

"Picture a stone falling into a still pond of water. The point at which the stone enters is an explosive splash, followed by powerful ripples traveling away from that point. As the ripples get farther from the entry point, they diminish in force and power."

The human body functions in much the same way, with the center of the body being the "splash point" and the strongest ripples being delivered from the torso. If you visit any training center, fit-

ness club or gym, you'll see a large percentage of the workload done sitting down and or lying down, inverting the core radiance formula. This is the opposite of what athletes want to do; it's also something anyone who wants to improve their quality of life long into old age should not do.

The first objective of core training is to develop the areas of the body that are responsible for the initiation and coordination of movement. Many training enthusiasts get

caught up in the use of a multitude of exercises involving the abdominal and low back muscles, mainly performed lying or sitting on the floor, or with a device. Just because you're specifically working the trunk or torso doesn't mean you're doing a "core" exercise. On the contrary, most standing exercises that involve a combination of flexion, extension and rotation are the better "core" exercises. Training with movements that constantly attend to proper posture, balance, stability and mobility (range of motion throughout the prescribed movement) will also involve the core, therefore almost all of the functional training performed by athletes is "core" training.

When analyzing your training exercises and drills, make sure that a great percentage (say, 85 to 90 percent) of your work truly involves the use of your core. Core strength has been shown to be the primary developmental building block. It must be in place before *absolute strength*, which is how we label the body's ability to

handle any load regardless of condition—this is basically just getting stronger. Next, we develop what we label as *relative strength*, or the body's ability to handle loads relative to body weight, in order to improve movement. This development should progress to more *dynamic strength*, the label for strength and speed combined (as in a jump for height). Finally, we develop *elastic strength*, or strength and speed with multiple rebound ability (as in bounding, hopping and sprinting). Understanding these strength

abilities and their development will help you progress into a more complete athlete.

The warm-up and beginning segments of each workout should emphasize specific work on the torso (trunk, shoulders and hips). A number of the exercises in your specialized workout (see Part 2) will work on improving hip mobility. Attending to this and core strength from the beginning will allow for more efficient progress in strength and speed, with diminished injury setbacks.

function of strength training

For the scope of this book, and as mentioned in the "Function of Core Training" section, strength is the ability to handle and move your body's weight, and any external loads necessary, for distances and speeds designated by competition, health and lifestyle. It's the ability to pull, squat or push the body against the forces of gravity for desired success.

The strength necessary to excel in a sport has different parameters than the strength necessary to do construction or climb a flight of stairs, and the strength needed by a distance runner is different than that of a wrestler. The objectives of functional strength training can be simple: to train the movements of pulling, squatting and pushing, and to perform the majority of exercises from a standing position in order to simulate the same postures, balance and stability

issues, and range of motions as in competitive athletic movements.

Pulling
Any athlete who has to start from a stationary position, jump or explode out of a stance performs pulling movements. If you closely observe a cyclist pedaling intensely, a sprinter in the blocks, or a field sport athlete defending an opponent, and then draw the stick figures of their positions, you'll find that their

positions will be the same as the figures pulling weight from the floor. Many practitioners think of pulling as all movements down or inward with the upper torso; however, athletic pulling begins with extension from the ground.

Squatting
Squatting movements can be viewed in a similar manner, with the addition of all-important hip rotation, which occurs when the hips are lowered below knee level. The objec-

tive of training with squats is to strengthen all of the muscles of the torso, hips and legs used in intense acceleration, sprinting, jumping, decelerating and changing direction. Many practitioners lower their hips to a position where some part of their thigh is parallel to the ground or their knee joint obtains a 90-degree angle, but this doesn't always result in true hip rotation nor engage all of the muscles that surround the hip.

Many coaches and practitioners say that sprinting and jumping do not require such an exaggerated hip range of motion. However, by not squatting fully, athletes neglect training the areas of the body that are used in highly com-petitive movement, as our work with the University of Oregon Strength & Conditioning Program and Exercise and Movement Science can attest. Over a fifteen-year period, in which the first seven was a constant battle to get athletes to achieve this squat position and posture, we collected data that showed increases in overall leg strength and power as well as noticeable decreases in lower back, hamstring and groin problems. Lunging and single-leg squatting also bring "function" to the leg-strengthening work. They mimic the movements of running and cutting while incorporating similar postures and stability issues, and strengthen the legs with less overall stress and intensity placed on the spine and torso.

Pushing

In terms of functional training, pushing movements must be done from a standing position. This is not intended to bash the bench press or other lying-down or sitting-down pushing movements, as they do have their place in training. However, pushing from a standing position requires more of the functions associated with athleticism. Pushing with an upright posture, altered balance, stabilized torso, mobility in the hips and shoulders, and moving the feet and legs into leveraged positions—these are athletic abilities to be improved with training.

Lowering the hips below knee level results in true hip rotation.

function of power training

The need for increased power (better utilization of what is available to the body; functional strength; directional speed and transitional agility) fits the profile of every athlete in some way. Even our experiences with ultra-marathoner's (50+ miles) and triathletes has shown us that this method of training for power can assist in the efficiency of each step, pedal or stroke, thereby aiding endurance by decreasing the amount of wasted movements and loss of energy from inefficient, less powerful movements.

Handling resistive overloads or gravity develops greater force production. Handling of temporal overloads, neuromuscularly and technically, and handling spatial overloads (involving movement in the sagittal, frontal and transverse planes) improve speed. This involves the distance quotient as well as several other aspects.

One aspect is anthropometry (differences in torso and limb length affect the ability to move efficiently through the optimal distance). The distance quotient involves mobility and agility and the abilities of movement through effective ranges that may involve efficient changes in direction. Coordination must also be

included to effectively summate the forces throughout the required distances with appropriate timing (Figure 3). Proper technique separates athletes who can apply power throughout the full use of their body from those who, due to limitations with technique, hinder their ability to be as powerful and effective as possible.

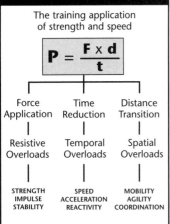

A POWER PERSPECTIVE

The training application
of strength and speed

$$P = \frac{F \times d}{t}$$

Force Application	Time Reduction	Distance Transition
Resistive Overloads	Temporal Overloads	Spatial Overloads
STRENGTH IMPULSE STABILITY	SPEED ACCELERATION REACTIVITY	MOBILITY AGILITY COORDINATION

Figure 3.

Basically, to increase athletic power, you need to:

1. Exhibit explosive strength and acceleration from a dead start.
2. Exhibit dynamic strength, coupling strength with speed and the use of countermovements (the stretch-shortening cycle).
3. Exhibit an elastic-reactive rebounding ability over multiple responses (more simply put, the ability to be more like a "super ball" rather than a tomato).

The improvement of starting strength and the ability to explosively accelerate from a dead stop is important in every field and court sport, the combative mat, the swimming pool and the cycling velodrome. Strength has its greatest value to an athlete when it can be exhibited at a rapid rate. Training improves this dynamic strength ability: "If you want to be fast, you must train fast." It's a bit more complicated than that, but not much. If all of your strength training has no dynamic or rapid movement component to it, then your ability to exhibit dynamic qualities competitively can be diminished.

Elastic-reactivity is simply the ability to rebound quickly from the ground with each powerful step, stride and bound, or from an object with a push, pull or countermove. Elastic strength is best demonstrated in repetitive motion (multiple responses).

The training programs that have the greatest amount of research and practical data on the improvement of these qualities are the explosive lifts, plyometric training, and the use of contrasting training, also known as "complex training" (see below).

Plyometrics

Plyometric exercises (pages 121–52) are a key component to increasing power by improving your ability to blend strength (forces of gravity), speed (rate of execution and ground contact time) and agility (the coordination of take-offs and flight in a multi-tude of directions)—and doing so merely with the use of your own body weight.

Among the concepts you'll find in this book are:

Skips The rhythm of skipping is one of a simple take-off and landing of the same foot. Step and take off with the right foot, land again on the right foot before stepping and landing on the left. This right-right, left-left, right-right, left-left rhythm can be applied to movements in all directions (forward, lateral and backward).

Jumps Attaining maximum height, or "projection of the hips upward," by involving both legs in the take-off and landing.

Bounds Gaining maximum horizontal distance, performed either with both feet together or in alternate fashion for the purposes of teaching and learning progressively and properly.

Twists Torquing and/or engaging in lateral movement of the torso.

Tosses/Passes Projecting movements of the upper torso and limbs that take place below and/or in front of the head.

Throws Projecting movements of the upper torso and limbs that occur above, over and/or across the head, signifying the difference between throwing and tossing/passing.

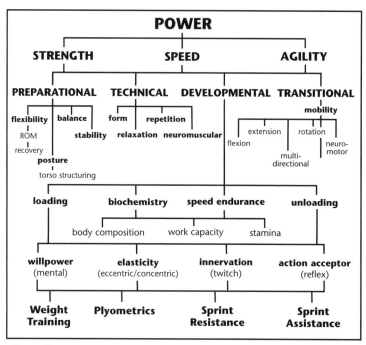

Figure 4.

Hops Achieving height and distance with a maximum rate of cyclic leg movement. With the complexity of hops early progressions use both legs for tall hip projection and cyclic leg action for all directions, then progressing to single-leg maneuvers.

Foundation Training and Progressions

If power is your ultimate goal, then you should place equal emphasis and attention on the combined effects of strength, speed and agility. In our model (Figure 4), we emphasize strength, speed and agility in a training session since they make up the whole of power. The *preparational portion* is basically warm-up. The *technical portion* of the training session is the transition from the effects of warm-up to more specific maneuvers in the realm of that session's skills (e.g., form running for speed sessions, bar routines for lifting sessions). The *developmental portion* is the "meat" of the day's session, the section dedicated to loading or unloading via weight training, jump training, sprint training, etc. The final segment of the session is tabbed the *transitional portion*. This is dedicated to improvement in transition-making, within oneself (flexion, extension and rotation), into the confines of one's field or court of play (from one point to another), or on to the next training session (recovery and/or restoration).

Contrasting Progressions

Complex training incorporates different training loads, speeds and styles in the quest for athletic power development. For instance, you might perform both strength and speed work in the same workout, or couple plyometric drills with heavy-resistance weight training.

For the purposes of this book, we'll use the following basic definitions for coupling our exercise selections:

Complexes = the execution of repetitions of 2 or more exercise styles within the same set (e.g., pull/push/squat x 3 =

3 pulls + 3 presses + 3 squats, or squat/jump x 3 = 3 squats + 3 jumps)

Combinations = the alternation of repetitions of 2 or more exercise styles within the same set (e.g., pull & squat & push x 3 = 1 pull + 1 squat + 1 push x 3)

Contrast = alternating heavy and light exercises set for set (e.g., squat/squat jump or speed squat = 3 x 80% / 3 x 35% / 3 x 85% / 3 x 35%)

Traditional = performing lighter resistance before the heavier resistance (e.g., graduating load sets = 3 x 70%, 3 x 80%, 3 x 85%...)

The rationale for the use of complex training is for improved utilization of time (workout session), utilization of space (floor, work, etc.) and utilization of equipment (barbells, dumbbells, etc.), as well as increased training volume, variety of workout and training cycles, and metabolic work capacity. A review of 14 research studies on this methodology found that 11 showed positive effects of complex training protocols, 2 offered no evidence that complex training protocols were effective, and 1 had negative training effects.

Participants need to work at high intensities in both the strength and speed portions of the complexes, at a volume that's low enough to guard against undue fatigue. The complex exercises should be biomechanically similar as well as multi-joint. Complex training may be utilized one to three times per week, allowing for adequate recovery (48 to 96 hours recommended). The timing of within-set rest periods has a wide range of suggestions. We recommend rest in the one- to four-minute range.

function of sprint training

The objective of sprint training is simple: to get from point A to point B faster. The sprint training drills in Part 3 are dedicated to improving your ability to run faster, more efficiently and in multiple directions.

Improving running speed has basic components, such as proper rhythm and cadence, and the coordination of muscle power. It requires intelligent training of proper form, relaxation, strength, endurance and flexibility. Relaxed, loose muscles move quickly, while tense, tight ones respond slowly.

The running drills on pages 153–71 are performed in a progressive order to develop sprinting skills in first an *acceleration* mode, then *speed* mode, and finally a *speed maintenance* mode, just as the order occurs in athletics. These drills also avoid movements that foster bad running

mechanics. The exclusion of hamstring curls, traditional butt kicks, and jogging is by design. Any exercise that encourages movement at the knee rather than at the hip just aids in the development of bad running mechanics— especially sprinting—and is avoided in this book.

Stride Length
Stride length is a large determining factor in increasing speed. Regardless of height, all fast people have a long, efficient stride. Without an effectively long stride it is difficult to run faster. Improving "Effective Stride Length"

(Figure 5), which is the projection of the hips (Seagrave & O'Donnell), results in the following:

- Increased strength/body weight ratio, the athlete being very strong and powerful in proportion to his/her body weight.
- Increased joint mobility— the greater the flexibility, the better the range of motion through which the athlete can exert the force.
- Development of greater coordination—the athlete can efficiently channel the strength and explosiveness into a more coordinated running form.

Figure 5.

When you watch fast runners, notice that they run tall or with their hips high, with a straight line of drive; the body leverage, or tilt of the torso, is aligned to transfer power. This must change, however, whenever changes of direction and quick cuts or reactions are performed. But for optimal acceleration and attainment of full speed, the body must be aligned straight and tall. Everything moves in a straight line, the feet do not point out, the arms do not cross the midline of the body. There is a high kick of the recovery leg. The shorter the lever, the faster the leg recovers each time (stride). The greater the knee drive upward and forward, the greater the force in the opposite direction on the driving leg, foot and ankle. In regards to arm action, the elbows drive at the shoulder with relaxed hands and forearms. The hands stay below shoulder level, with the thumbs up to aid the elbows in pumping backward with recovery forward, not across the body.

Points of Emphasis

Sprint with your ankle locked, as if your toes were trying to scratch your knees; explode from your foot and ankle as much as you can. This toe-up rule spring-loads the ankle and lessens ground contact time.

Your knees should generate powerful thrusts upward and forward. Make sure they drive in the desired direction. There should be good, complete extension of the back (support) leg to accompany good knee drive, in addition to maximum elbow pump backwards; this maximizes the length throughout the acceleration.

Your motion should be in a direct line (forward and not up) or to the angle you choose to turn. Your shoulders should stay square to the direction of the goal; make sure your shoulders and neck are relaxed to allow optimal elbow pump and an erect trunk. Your head should be held erect and relaxed, with your eyes focused on the goal. Your lower lip and cheeks should bounce as you move.

The drills and progressions in Part 3 (pages 153–71) are a simplified manner in which to achieve the above objectives. They are broken down into three main areas:

1) **The ability to start from a complete stop and project the hips immediately in any direction.** Clinical and practical evaluation supports the concept that any and all good starts are the result of eliminating false steps and pushing into the ground so the hips move immediately in the desired direction.

THE TEN COMMANDMENTS OF FAST RUNNING

1. Understand that execution is based upon relaxation and focus.
2. Realize that the quality of the neuromuscular coordination comes before the quantity of strength and power.
3. Train for technique before speed development.
4. Emphasize specific development of coordinated fast movements.
5. Utilize exercises and drills that are specific to the desired results.
6. Remember that stride length is more readily developable than stride frequency.
7. Recognize that "effective stride length" is hip projection and the ratio of strength and power over body weight.
8. Acknowledge that speed and strength are most productive when speed is superior to strength.
9. Know that speed development comes before speed endurance.
10. Embrace the fact that speed is a long, dedicated and consistent refinement process.

"A" AND "B" SERIES

There is often controversy on the use of the "A" (toe up/knee up, thigh acceleration) and "B" (toe/knee/heel-up re-acceleration) series for sprint training (see pages 158–62), derived from the Gerard Mach sequence. Often used for a variety of technique work, warm-up routines, and form running, the "A" and "B" drills focus on the muscles that you sprint with and train them in that manner without having to do repeated, full-out sprints. They are not form and technique drills by design. You can improve acceleration technique sooner and more consistently by the use of resistance such as hills and sleds. Using the B series for technique work can often bog down the learning curve rather than assist it. The best use of these drills is for training sprinting more often. They can be used in a warm-up situation, on off days from heavy conditioning or as rehabilitation and recovery training from injuries to the hamstring, hip flexor, groin, and low back since a good portion of these injuries have come from weakness in the hips, and overstriding. If you just treat and strengthen the sore or strained hamstring then rehabilitate with jogging, once you start sprinting again, the main causes for pulls and strains have not been addressed. Get them back into sprint shape via the use of these drills.

2) **The ability to accelerate effectively.** This is also the elimination of false steps that land out in front of the hip and knee. The mechanics of acceleration are *push* mechanics. The foot lands fully with the weight over the front half. The shin is angled forward (positive) over the mid-foot. The push is down and actively back. Do not just let the foot fall.

3) **The ability to transition into another gear (e.g., deceleration, change of direction).** On the occasion it is a higher gear (high speed), this involves the elimination of pull mechanics and overstriding, and the use of *paw* mechanics with proper cycling and recovery of the leg.

Starting Positions

Two- and three-point sprint starts (pages 153–57) are a progression of explosive take-offs from four main positions. The progression always begins with a two-point stance (where the only two points on the ground are both feet) to develop balance, take-off stability, and the elimination of the false step. Once a three-point stance (both feet plus one hand in contact with the ground) is assumed, these skills are alleviated or often deteriorate. The power production of a three-point start can be greatly enhanced if two-point stances are trained. Starts from the varied two-point stances help to train cutting movements in change of direction situations. Starts should concentrate on the first three to five steps.

The three most important concepts of these starts are:

- The initial push-off should be made with both feet.
- The torso must be set rigidly from hips through shoulders.
- The lead steps must be quick and direct to drive the hips directionally.

The stances on pages 153–57 are a part of true athletic movements in sports that require a stationary starting position (tennis and other racquet sports, football, baseball and softball, volleyball, goalies in net sports, basketball, soccer, and both field and ice hockey). These are also progressions to positions that aid in the change of direction principles described in the agility section (page 21).

Two-point stance.

Three-point stance.

function of agility training

Training for functional agility involves the ability to change body position, position on a field or course of play, and/or avoid obstacles rapidly and accurately without losing balance. Most practitioners agree that this is dependent upon muscular power, coordination, mobility and reactive abilities.

The objectives of enhancing agility are very clear cut. First, improve the ability to change direction at high speeds. Second, understand that it's basically the ability to "turn and run." Running into and out of direction changes, which we will label "breaks" or "cuts," can be broken down into two simple maneuvers: speed cuts and power cuts.

Speed cuts involve being able to break without deceleration, hence without slowing down considerably. They are direction changes of lesser angles, planting off of the inside, or direction side, foot. The crossover step (page 154) is a lead-in to this move. *Power cuts* involve major deceleration and then re-acceleration, planting off of the outside foot and breaking into greater angle directions. The power cut requires considerable dynamic strength, posture and stability in order to plant and cut without false-stepping in a direction anywhere but underneath the hip. Hip projection as practiced by the open step (page 154) and drop step (page 155) starts are lead-ins to the power cut moves.

In much of the University of Oregon Strength & Conditioning Program and Exercise and Movement Science's experience and data collection, we have found simple answers to the debate on whether a crossover is better than an open step, or vice versa. In novice performers, the crossover step has shown faster initial get-off. Video analysis reveals that without practice they push off with both feet and project the hips better than unpracticed open steps. The hips are often held higher as with higher-velocity running and speed cuts. In many sports, however, the crossover step can lead to improper positions on the field or court. Crossover technique may also lead to step sequences that are not as efficient as open technique due to other change-of-direction needs. Once trained in the art of projecting the hips from the open technique, the get-off times become more comparable, and may be more useful in certain positions and patterns on the field or court. The same analogy can be made for the backward turn-and-run options. In this situation, the pivot step (page 155) not only has the same pattern and position issues as the crossover, it has not been shown to be faster in any of our initial get-off studies. This again is mainly due to an inability to project the hips immediately in the desired direction.

Open Step

Crossover Step

Drop Step

Pivot Step

before you begin

This book is intended for individuals of a wide range of ages and abilities. Since the book is progressive in nature, you should be able to begin with the initial exercises; as you become more comfortable with them, you can move onward. With this in mind, the only prerequisites are to get physical clearance from a medical doctor or orthopedist, just as any sports program requires of its athletes.

Stance

When initiating most powerful movements, you'll want to have a proper stance. Placing your feet directly under your hips will ensure good biomechanical force production from your feet up through your torso; wider stances, on the other hand, inhibit power initiation. Your torso must be erect, with your back flat or arched, your chest spread forward and your hips cocked backward. Standing with your hips tucked under and your back rounded leads to mushy postures and perform-ances, as you can easily see—poor torso posture doesn't even look powerful. Your feet should maintain full contact with the ground while you keep your knees flexed. Shift your weight over the front half of your feet, but not to the point where your heels leave the ground. The inability to keep your heels on the ground as you bend your knees is a sure sign that both take-offs and landings will be a problem until flexibility is improved. Any stance that would be used to jump high in the air is the same for powerful movements in a multitude of directions.

Tools

The largest aspect of training with a "functional mentality" is the use of different tools, or equipment, to help foster the acquisition of skills. Anything from A–Z, from barbells to wobble boards, can be used to develop athletic abilities. Many would agree that oftentimes practitioners "lose the forest for the trees" in their quest for training functionally. For some it becomes more about the

tools or gadgets than it is about the biomechanical skills and aspects of performance.

The objective of *Functional Training* is to pass on as much of the technical mastery of athletic performance, utilizing some tools, such as for strength training, yet attending to the actual movements more than specialized tools that aid the movements. This statement should not be taken to imply that many and most of the tools are not in some way useful. It is just an approach similar to the context of the athletic performances themselves.

The tools used in this book

include: barbells, dumbbells, medicine balls, cones, plyo boxes, and elastic strapping.

Preventing Injury

Articles in periodicals such as *Medicine & Science in Sport & Exercise* and the *American Journal of Sports Medicine* continually give us plenty of information on the causes of and possible relief from many types of problems that occur in and around sport and training for sport. Research in the area of rehabilitation and preventative measures (some suggest the term "pre-habilitation") for these types of

injuries has also increased, as has the amount of preventative training.

If we look closely at the parameters with which we assess injuries and subsequently administer treatment and training, we should see a pattern (Figure 6). Providing the protocols for treatment and training use a progressive nature, in which the functionality of both are very closely matched. Consider an adage once proposed by Barry Bates, a wise University of Oregon biomechanist: "All injury is the result of change, likewise, all healing is the result of change." The message then, is that proper progressions along the functional path of training can prepare you for changes that, at the most, can keep you from getting injured, or, at the very least, help you to recover sooner.

This book is designed with these issues in mind. The

TREATMENT & TRAINING		
Functional Methodologies		
Eccentric Injury	**Treatment**	**Training**
Force	Lengthening	Resistive
Length Change	Loading	Spatial
Length Velocity	Contraction Speed	Temporal

Figure 6.

exercises are laid out in the proper progressions, from the simple exercises to the more complex, so that you can learn and execute the proper mechanics of flexing, extending and rotating about the torso in order to develop the ability to land and take-off properly in a multitude of directions. If you train in the order prescribed by your specialized workout in Part 2, and if you progress through the exercises and drills, mastering the proper postures, balance issues, and stability/mobility needs, you'll begin to notice enhanced performance and the stamina involved with safer, healthier training.

Things to Look Out For

Monitor proper technique by evaluating the posture, balance, stability and mobility/flexibility of each exercise performance. Is the exercise performed with an upright posture, balanced over the instep of the foot, stabilized through the joints involved, and with the proper range of motion? If not, backtrack, master these skills and then progress.

Obviously, exercises performed on both feet are simpler than those that are on one, and traveling at angles is more complex than moving in place. For example, avoid moving on to a plyometric exercise (bounds or hops) that has you landing on one leg if you have not mastered the proper landing/take-off posture nor the balance needed for quick and explosive two-legged landings (jumping).

Progress from single-response movements, where you perform one repetition, check the posture, balance, stability and mobility of that rep, and then repeat. Progress to multiple response with a pause, in which you perform several repetitions in succession, pausing to assess technical mastery, then repeat without resetting. Finally, progress to multiple responses or the execution of repetitions in succession and at maximum rate. The key to performance of multiple repetitions is being in take-off position prior to landing, minimizing the time on the ground and maximizing force development.

Master the proper extension of the torso in a clean pull before attempting to seriously train the clean-and-jerk combination, since the inability to finish the pull leads to other issues of poor performance and possible injury.

part two:

the

programs

how to use this book

This section of *Functional Training* presents workouts for a wide range of sports, such as baseball, wrestling, biking, basketball and gymnastics. In order to choose the best one for your goals, you must first evaluate your sport and the movements involved.

Evaluating the elements of athleticism is necessary in improving the planning and performance of training and, therefore, competition. Vern Gambetta writes that a failure to completely assess the demands of your sport manifests itself later as performance errors, injuries or overtraining. Consider the elements of the sport(s) you are conditioning for.

1. Is there contact (especially with the ground) or collision? What are the rules? How do the rules apply to the length of game, length of rest periods, length of playing surface and width of playing surface?

2. Is the percentage of flight vertical (e.g., volleyball) or horizontal (e.g., football)? Is time in the air (running or jumping) a negative or positive aspect of performance? Are there a series of one- or two-foot take-offs and/or landings?

3. How do you get from point A to point B? We often assume that a great deal more lateral movement takes place than often does. How much do you "turn and run"? How far do you accelerate before you start decelerating?

4. What skill is needed for you to truly perform well? A simple way to analyze this aspect is by observing the hips. Do the skills require movement at, and projection of, the hips? You might be doing a lot of training for the sake of footwork, quickness, mobility, etc., that eludes these two extremely important aspects. Does the movement of the feet help to effectively project the hips in the direction they need to go? Can the skill be effectively performed without quality movement at and about the hips?

Now analyze the practicality of the drills that you do or have done in training for your sport. Does the drill fit the skill? We often perform drill work to take up time, so to speak. The drill is fun and enjoyable but often doesn't accomplish the goal of improving a skill needed on the competition surface. Over the course of valuable training time, the participants get much better at the drill, but not necessarily better at the skill. We see this often with sprint drills using mini-hurdles, for instance. They may have some value in teaching or getting a feel for certain mechanics, but they might not accomplish the actual goal of improving quality hip projection in acceleration, or recovery mechanics in speed.

A better understanding of biomechanics will help you to apply the right movements to the skills and the right drills to accomplish the movements. Are you using the correct foot placement? Is your torso tilted correctly, enabling your landings and take-offs to be immediate and precise? Do you bend down or bend over to change direction? The ability to assess these questions, answer them and work towards applying the answers to training skills, drills and overall development is the key to improving performance.

The Workouts

The drills in each of the following workouts are presented in a progressive manner so that you first learn the building blocks of functional movement. The sequences, cues and performance protocols will be your guide to moving on to the next level of exercises.

Before moving on to the program for your sport, be sure to do the Dynamic Warm-Up, Core Training, Strength Training and Power Training workouts as noted.

The *Dynamic Warm-Up* (page 34), designed to increase technical mobility, should be performed entirely and religiously each and every training day. Different routines can be utilized, as long as all of the drill areas are covered (e.g. forward, lateral, backward, walk, crawl, etc.).

Follow up the warm-up with the *Core Training* program (page 35), which will strengthen as well as improve the body's ability to move in all planes of direction. The core routine should include 10 to 12 of the listed exercises each workout day. One dozen takes about 10 minutes to perform.

For the *Strength Training* program (page 36), do one to three exercises from the pulling, squatting and pushing sections during each training session. This might involve one major pull or squat (e.g., Clean, Front Squat) and one or two minor exercises (e.g., Good Morning, Step-Up with Push-Off).

These three workouts should be done three alternating days per week for the first four phases of training. Monday/Wednesday/Friday are common practice days, but any and all days of the week can work as long as you take a day of recovery in between. For example, Tuesday/Thursday/Saturday work just as well.

The *Power Training* program (page 37) should be performed with two to three days of recovery in between (e.g., Monday and Friday).

After you've performed these three workouts as prescribed, you're ready to tackle your sport-specific workout (pages 38–56). The plyometric drills progress in two ways, the first by complexity. The simple ones are performed for several weeks as more complex ones are added; eventually you move away from the simple ones, but not until you have properly mastered them. The second progression is by impact, so first you perform the drills landing on two legs and without traveling, then the drills that take off from one leg and land on another (bounding), and then finally those that travel on one leg only (hopping). For all progressions, remember that you must attain mastery of proper posture, balance, stability and mobility before moving to a more complex and/or higher impact exercise.

The speed and agility drills should be performed on a consistent basis as you continue to improve how your nervous system adapts to the proper techniques and rate of movement requirements.

program planning

Exercise program planning is simply creating a map to a certain fitness and competition destination. It's the practical way of getting to your desired goals and objectives safely and efficiently. Think of driving. In most cases when you get in a car, you have a destination picked out.

The store, the office, the beach, whatever it may be, you know where you want to go, and know how to get there. From experience, you know the best ways to get to the store: which streets to avoid, when to make turns. On rare occasions you may not have a destination in mind, so you drive around aimlessly. On other occasions, you may want to get to a better destination, a bigger store or a nicer beach. In these instances, you need a good map.

Training for success in athletic endeavors is the same. You must have a destination in mind. A destination can be a championship, or the accomplishment of certain goals and objectives (such as fitness and durability) within the process of getting there. Whatever the destination, proper program planning is the continual process of making the right map to get you there. The reason we say continual process is because no plan is completely perfect—rarely can the same plan get the exact same results. It's much like the drive to the store, where you won't always get the same light changes and same pedestrians. A good plan needs to be continually adjusted so that you can still be able to arrive at your destination safely and efficiently.

An old axiom of track distance coaches is "plan the race, then race the plan." Failing in the race first comes from not having a plan. Secondly, whether the plan is a good one or not—just as whether or not the new road map is good—will not be discovered unless you use it. Turn when the map says to turn, take the roads the map has laid out. Failure to race the plan is the same as not having a plan. Failure from racing the plan, however, has a positive aspect: It gives you something to work with and learn from, to improve the map to the destination. If the plan is never raced or the map not used properly, then we'll never know where we failed; our ability to get to the destination becomes much more difficult.

We know it's important to have a destination. Now, where do you want to go? Once you decide, you must devise a good map. What plan is most likely to lead you in the desired direction? In other words, what type of training will enable you to accomplish your objective? The following guidelines—map-making skills, so to speak—are broken down from long term to short term. These will hopefully provoke you to think about where you want to go and how best to get there.

Yearly

Planning the year can be very complicated or fairly simple. There are two main points to consider when planning a year-round program:

1) When is the ultimate destination (e.g., Olympic Games, state championship, big race)? Where in the year do you need to be your fittest physically, physiologically and psychologically?

2) Are you training to qualify and then compete in a finale, or are you training for success over a long, hard season in order to reach an ultimate destination?

Once you've decided where the "pot o' gold," or that ulti-mate success place, in the year is, you can work backwards from there. Split the year into several sections, three or four work best. The section that leads up to and contains the ultimate destination is the "in-season" or *competitive period*. The section before that is the "pre-season" or *pre-competitive period*. The section of the year completely opposite the competitive section is the "off-season" or *preparatory period*, just as the one immediately after the in-season is aptly called the "post-season" or *transition period*. Each section, or training period, has slightly different objectives, all of them being progressive parts of your big plan. Athletes who try to train for the championship the same way all year-round tend to create chronic health and performance problems.

Seasonally

Once you've broken down the year into seasons, you can further segment each one of these periods into fairly consistent phases of training. Each period, regardless of where in the year it is, will have some basic components. Each training period should include a preparatory work phase, a maximum work phase, a power conversion phase and a maintenance/evaluative phase.

The *preparatory work phase* will generally last one to four weeks depending on the shape you're in. The build-up phases in the post- and off-seasons usually last two to four weeks, whereas the pre- and in-season should be shorter.

Follow the prep work with the *maximum work phase*, with some type of maximum efforts, intensities, and/or durations. The duration of this phase should not exceed four weeks. Breakdowns can result in injury and future problems if the training exceeds four or more weeks. The late Bill Bowerman would suggest many years ago, when training distance runners, that more is not better, and to keep things in 14-, 21- or, at the very most, 28-day training cycles.

Following the maximum training phase will be a phase where you'll convert to either more power emphasis or, possibly in the case of long-distance athletes (marathoner, triathlete, cyclist, etc.), more duration emphasis. This *power conversion phase* will be geared toward the functional emphasis of this book, and the specificity of most athletic endeavors. This is another phase you want to limit to four weeks. You may choose to alternate max phases and power phases if your training period or off-

	Preparational ——→		Evaluative/Competitive	
Strength Training Phases	Build-up Adaptive	Maximum Strength	Conversion to Power or Endurance	Maintenance
	Preparational ——→		Evaluative/Competitive	
Speed Training Phases	Acceleration	Speed	Speed Endurance	Specific Maintenance
	Preparational ——→		Evaluative/Competitive	
Plyometric Training Phases	Begin progressions JUMP TOSS	BOUND HOP THROW	Combos & "Shock" Methods	Maintenance Routines
	Preparational ——→		Evaluative/Competitive	
Agility Training Phases	Posture Balance Stability Mobility progressions	Speed & Power Cut Specifics	Reactionary Changes of Direction	Specific Sport Drills

Seasonal Plans

THE PERIODS

- A blend of guidelines that progress equally and efficiently through the training and competing periods
- Progressions that graduate in technique complexity, impact intensity, and competition-specific volumes and durations

Bompa 1983,
Pfaff 1993,
Radcliffe 1998

Figure 7.

season is lengthy. Usually, one or two 21- to 28-day cycles of each can take up the majority of a training period.

Finish off the seasonal period with some sort of *maintenance* or *evaluation of training and/or competition*. This will vary with the seasons as well. During the in-season, the maintenance phase, emphasizing practice and competition rather than training improvement, can be fairly long, as opposed to the post-, off- or pre-seasons, which can have little or no such phase.

Monthly

Each two- to four-week training phase can now be looked at as a variety of training methods that can progress you through each season. The guidelines can be broken down into specific training methods. Specific examples for different sports and activities appear in the sport-specific workout programs; an example of more specific training phase objectives methods are illustrated in Figure 7. The main concept behind the phases of training is to progress toward goals with both consistency and variety for a healthier, comprehensive training approach.

Weekly

While the monthly phases of training stress changing up the various modes, the weekly cycles of training emphasize consistency. Within each training phase, you might have two to three weeks (14- to 21-day cycles) of training which will feature exercises and methods that are the same from week to week. Each week can be increased in dosage (either by volume and/or intensity), and the success of handling these increases is monitored for effective progress. The fourth week can be a further evaluation of the success of the progress made over the three-week cycle. Figure 8 shows an example of progressive weekly dosages. Simple tests such as Vertical Jump, Standing Long Jump, and/or Medicine Ball Throws performed at the beginning of each week, or extensively during week four, help to determine success in

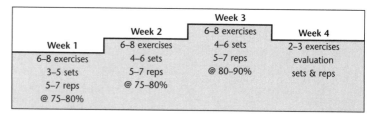

Figure 8.

recovery and continued power development.

Daily

The key to success comes not just from what to do each day, but when and why. The daily session should start with great consistency, and can end with more variety. For example, the warm-up should be standard, with two or three different routines. The warm-up is comprehensive, however; keeping the daily choices to a minimum will help the athlete to keep the routine consistent. The technical portion, that transition from general to core preparation, should be consistently matched to the specifics of the main training for that day. The main training portion should be consistent to the goals and objectives of the month's training phase. The transition section or the end of each session can change to help expand the agility, mobility and flexibility comfort zones of the athlete.

The following chart is an example of training sessions based upon a one-hour menu:

TIME	WEIGHT ROOM SETTING	CONDITIONING FIELD SETTING
:00	**Preparational Period** • Dynamic Warm-Up *Target:* Abdominals & low back	**Preparational Period** • Dynamic Warm-Up *Target:* flexion/extension/rotation
:11	**Technical Period** • Core specifics, postural pulling, squatting, pushing with light bar/stick	**Technical Period** • Form walk, skip, run, prance, gallop (forward, lateral and backward)
:21	**Developmental Period** • Main lifting sequence of circuit, stage, general, maximum, dynamic, and/or elastic strength training	**Developmental Period** • Main sequence of plyometric, sprint resistance/assistance, and/or speed endurance work
:46	**Mobility Period** • Specific training involving resistance loads and footwork, squat jumps, medicine ball presses and throws, split snatches, dumbbell drills, slide board, etc.	**Mobility Period** • Drills and games using speed cuts and power cuts, situation starts, timed change of direction, etc.
:56	**Cool Down**	**Cool Down**

• Barefoot Striding
• Backward Running
• Static, AIS and PNF stretching

DYNAMIC WARM-UP – All Sports

mode				*all phases
walking		p. 60	Top o' the Head Drill—Knee Grab	1 x 10–12
		p. 61	Top o' the Head Drill—Froggie	1 x 10–12
		p. 62	Top o' the Head Drill—March	1 x 10–12
		p. 63	Heel Walk	1 x 10–12
		p. 64	Toe Walk	1 x 10–12
		p. 65	Toe Grab	1 x 10–20
lunging		p. 66	Forward Lunge	1 x 4–8
		p. 67	Side-to-Side Lunge	1 x 4–8
		p. 66	Backward Lunge	1 x 4–8
crawling		p. 68	Hands & Heels	1 x 10–12
		p. 68	Mountain Climb	1 x 10–12
skipping		p. 69	Exaggerated Skip	1 x 10–20
		p. 69	Crossover Skip	1 x 10–20
laterals		p. 70	Shuffle	2 x 10–20
		p. 71	Lateral Skip	2 x 10–20
		p. 72	Carioca	2 x 10–20
backwards		p. 73	Backward Run	1 x 10–20
		p. 74	Backpedal	1 x 10–20
		p. 75	Backward Skip	1 x 10–20
		p. 76	Backward Shuffle	1 x 10–20

* phase 1 = weeks 1–3   **phase 2** = weeks 4–6   **phase 3** = weeks 7–9   **phase 4** = weeks 10–12

CORE TRAINING – All Sports

mode   *all phases

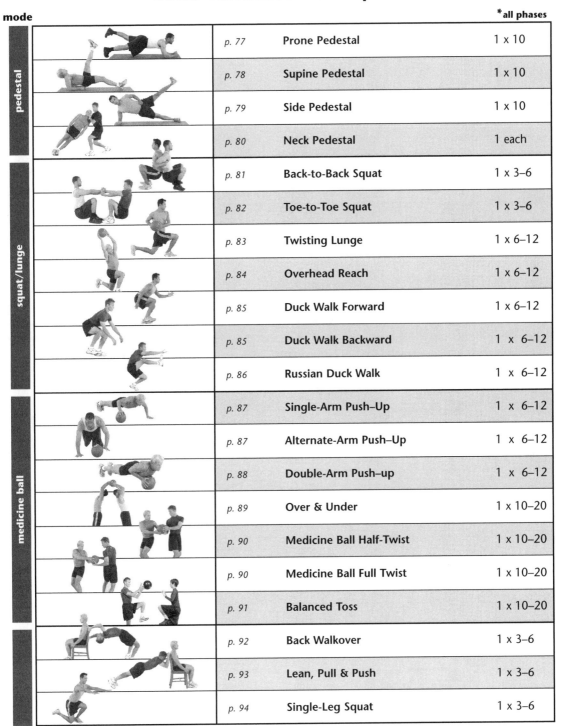

pedestal	*p. 77*	Prone Pedestal	1 x 10
	p. 78	Supine Pedestal	1 x 10
	p. 79	Side Pedestal	1 x 10
	p. 80	Neck Pedestal	1 each
squat/lunge	*p. 81*	Back-to-Back Squat	1 x 3–6
	p. 82	Toe-to-Toe Squat	1 x 3–6
	p. 83	Twisting Lunge	1 x 6–12
	p. 84	Overhead Reach	1 x 6–12
	p. 85	Duck Walk Forward	1 x 6–12
	p. 85	Duck Walk Backward	1 x 6–12
	p. 86	Russian Duck Walk	1 x 6–12
medicine ball	*p. 87*	Single-Arm Push–Up	1 x 6–12
	p. 87	Alternate-Arm Push–Up	1 x 6–12
	p. 88	Double-Arm Push–up	1 x 6–12
	p. 89	Over & Under	1 x 10–20
	p. 90	Medicine Ball Half-Twist	1 x 10–20
	p. 90	Medicine Ball Full Twist	1 x 10–20
	p. 91	Balanced Toss	1 x 10–20
	p. 92	Back Walkover	1 x 3–6
	p. 93	Lean, Pull & Push	1 x 3–6
	p. 94	Single-Leg Squat	1 x 3–6

STRENGTH TRAINING – All Sports

mode					Phase 1	Phase 2	Phase 3
pulling			p. 95	Good Morning	3 x 6–10	3 x 6–10	3 x 6–10
			p. 96	Stiff-Leg Deadlift	3 x 6–10	3 x 6–10	3 x 6–10
			p. 97	Russian Deadlift	3 x 6–10	3 x 6–10	3 x 6–10
			p. 98	Clean Pull	3 x 6–10	4 x 3–6	2 x 4–8
			p. 99	High Pull	3 x 3–6	4 x 3–5	5 x 2–4
squatting			p. 100	Overhead Squat	3 x 6–10	2 x 4–8	3 x 6–10
			p. 101	Overhead Lunge	3 x 6–10	2 x 4–8	3 x 6–10
			p. 102	Front Squat	4 x 4–8	4 x 4–8	4 x 4–8
	not pictured		p. 102	Front Lunge	4 x 4–8	2 x 4–8	2 x 4–8
	not pictured		p. 102	Back Squat	4 x 4–8	4 x 4–8	4 x 4–8
			p. 102	Back Lunge	2 x 4–8	2 x 4–8	4 x 4–8
			p. 103	Step-Up Slow	4 x 4	4 x 4	4 x 4
			p. 104	Step-Up w/Push–Off	3 x 6–8	3 x 6–8	3 x 6–8
			p. 105	Step-Up w/Knee Drive	3 x 6–8	3 x 6–8	3 x 6–8
			p. 106	Step-Up Fast		3 x 12	3 x 12
			p. 107	Step-Down	3 x 5	3 x 5	3 x 5
			p. 108	Single-Leg Squat (Loaded)		3 x 3–6	3 x 3–6
pushing			p. 109	Overhead Press	3 x 6–10	2 x 6–10	2 x 6–10
			p. 110	Push Press	3 x 4–8	2 x 4–6	4 x 4–8
			p. 111	Push Jerk	4 x 3–5	2 x 2–4	4 x 3–5
			p. 112	Split Jerk		4 x 2–4	4 x 2–4

* phase 1 = weeks 1–3   **phase 2** = weeks 4–6   **phase 3** = weeks 7–9   **phase 4** = weeks 10–12

POWER TRAINING – All Sports

node				Phase 1	Phase 2	Phase 3
olympic lifts		p. 114	Snatch		5 x 2–4	5 x 2–4
		p. 116	Clean		5 x 2–4	3 x 2–4
		p. 118	Clean & Jerk		4 x 1–3	5 x 1–3
		p. 120	Squat Jump (Loaded)		4 x 2–4	4 x 2–4

PLYOMETRICS

MODE	EXERCISE	BASEBALL / SOFTBALL				BASKETBALL			
		*phase 1	phase 2	phase 3	phase 4	*phase 1	phase 2	phase 3	phase 4
Jumping	Pogo, p. 121	3x8-12	3x8-12			3x8-12	3x8-12	3x8-12	
Jumping	Squat Jump, p. 122	3x3-6	3x3-6	3x3-6		3x3-6	3x3-6	3x3-6	3x3-6
Jumping	Double-Leg Slide Kick, p. 123	3x8-12	3x8-12	3x8-12	3x3-6	3x3-6	3x3-6	3x3-6	3x3-6
Jumping	Knee Tuck Jump, p. 124		3x3-6	3x3-6	3x3-6		3x3-6	3x3-6	3x3-6
Jumping	Split Jump, p. 125		2x4-8	2x4-8	2x4-8		2x4-8	2x4-8	2x4-8
Jumping	Scissor Jump, p. 126		2x6-12	2x6-12	2x6-12		2x6-12	2x6-12	2x6-12
Jumping	Depth Jump, p. 127				1x4-6				1x4-6
Bounding	Prance, p. 128	3x8-12	3x8-12	3x8-12	3x3-6	3x8-12	3x8-12	3x8-12	3x3-6
Bounding	Gallop, p. 129	2x8-12	2x8-12	2x8-12	3x3-6	2x8-12	2x8-12	2x8-12	3x3-6
Bounding	Fast Skip, p. 130	3x8-12	3x8-12	3x8-12	3x3-6	3x8-12	3x8-12	3x8-12	3x3-6
Bounding	Power Skip, p. 130		3x3-6	3x3-6	3x3-6		3x3-6	3x3-6	3x3-6
Bounding	Ankle Flip, p. 131		2x8-12	2x8-12	3x8-12		2x8-12	2x8-12	3x8-12
Bounding	Bounding, p. 132			2x8-12	2x8-12			2x8-12	2x8-12
Bounding	Lateral Bounding, p. 133				2x8-12				2x8-12
Hopping	Double-Leg Hops, p. 134	3x3-6	3x3-6	3x3-6	3x3-6	3x3-6	3x3-6	3x3-6	3x3-6
Hopping	Side Hops, p. 135	3x3-6	3x3-6	3x3-6	3x3-6	3x3-6	3x3-6	3x3-6	3x3-6
Hopping	Single-Leg Pogo, p. 136			3x3-6	3x3-6			3x3-6	3x3-6
Hopping	Single-Leg Slide Kick, p. 137				3x3-6				3x3-6
Hopping	Single-Leg Hops, p. 138				3x3-6				3x3-6
Hopping	Diagonal Hops, p. 139				3x3-6				3x3-6
Hopping	Lateral Hops, p. 140				3x3-6				3x3-6
Tosses/Throws	Shovel Toss, p. 141	2x5	2x5	2x5		2x5	2x5	2x5	
Tosses/Throws	Scoop Toss, p. 142	2x5	2x5	2x5		2x5	2x5	2x5	
Tosses/Throws	Twist Toss, p. 143	2x6	2x6	2x6		2x6	2x6	2x6	
Tosses/Throws	Scoop Throw, p. 144			2x5	2x5			2x5	2x5
Tosses/Throws	Diagonal Throw, p. 145			2x6	2x6			2x6	2x6
Tosses/Throws	Kneeling Forward Throw, p. 146	1x5	1x5	1x5			1x5	1x5	2x5
Tosses/Throws	Standing Forward Throw, p. 147	1x5	1x5	1x5	1x5		1x5	1x5	2x5
Tosses/Throws	Stepping Forward Throw, p. 148	1x5	1x5	1x5	1x5		1x5	1x5	2x5
Push-Ups	Wall Push-Up, p. 149	2x5	2x5			2x5	2x5		
Push-Ups	Drop Push-Up, p. 150			2x5	2x5			2x5	2x5
Push-Ups	Kneeling Chest Pass, p. 151	2x5	2x5			2x5	2x5		
Push-Ups	Chest Pass, p. 152			2x5	2x5			2x5	2x5

Category	Exercise	Phase 1 (wks 1–3)	Phase 2 (wks 4–6)	Phase 3 (wks 7–9)	Phase 4 (wks 10–12)
COMPLEXES	Good Morning/Overhead Press/Overhead Squat, pp. 95, 109, 100	3x5–8	3x5–8	3x5–8	3x5–8
	Front Squat/Jerk, pp. 102, 118	5x2–4	5x2–4	5x2–4	5x2–4
	Power Clean/Scoop Toss, pp. 117, 142	3x2–4	3x2–4	3x2–4	3x2–4
	Lunge/Split Jump, pp. 66, 125	2x4–8	2x4–8	2x4–8	2x4–8
COMBOS	Clean & Jerk, p. 118	4x1–3	4x1–3	4x1–3	4x1–3
	Front Squat & Jerk, pp. 102, 118	4x1–3	4x1–3	4x1–3	4x1–3
	Overhead Press/Overhead Squat, pp. 109, 100	3x5–8	3x5–8	3x5–8	3x5–8
	Clean & Front Squat & Jerk, pp. 116, 102, 118	4x1–3	4x1–3	4x1–3	4x1–3
SPRINT TRAINING — Starts	Squared Step, p. 153	2x/leg	2x/leg	2x/leg	2x/leg
	Staggered Step, p. 153	2x/side	2x/side	2x/side	2x/side
	Open Step, p. 154	2x/side	2x/side	2x/side	2x/side
	Crossover Step, p. 154	2x/side	2x/side	2x/side	2x/side
	Drop Step, p. 155	2x/side	2x/side	2x/side	2x/side
	Pivot Step, p. 155	2x/side	2x/side	2x/side	2x/side
	Balanced Starts, p. 156	2x/side	2x/side	2x/side	2x/side
	Resisted Starts, p. 157	2x/side	2x/side	2x/side	2x/side
Acceleration	"A" Walk, p. 158	2x20yds	2x20yds	2x20yds	2x20yds
	"A" Skip, p. 158	2x20yds	2x20yds	2x20yds	2x20yds
	Wall Drill, p. 160	2x6–10	2x6–10	2x6–10	2x6–10
	"A" Run (Slide kick), p. 158	2x20yds	2x20yds	2x20yds	2x20yds
Speed	"B" Walk, p. 161	2x20yds	2x20yds	2x20yds	2x20yds
	"B" Skip, p. 161	2x20yds	2x20yds	2x20yds	2x20yds
	Cadence Fast Leg, p. 162	2x20yds	2x20yds	2x20yds	2x30yds
AGILITY	Sit Drill, p. 163	1x6	1x6	1x6	1x6
	Sway Drill, p. 164	1x6	1x6	1x6	1x6
	Speed Weave, p. 166	4–6x	4–6x	4–6x	4–6x
	Shuttle Run, p. 167	4–6x	4–6x	4–6x	4–6x
	Power Weave, p. 168	4–6x	4–6x	4–6x	4–6x
	3-Cone "L" Run, p. 169	4–6x	4–6x	4–6x	4–6x
	Directional Drill, p. 170	4–6x	4–6x	4–6x	4–6x

PLYOMETRICS

MODE	BICYCLING				EXERCISE	GOLF			
	*phase 1	phase 2	phase 3	phase 4		*phase 1	phase 2	phase 3	phase 4
Jumping	3x8-12	3x8-12			Pogo, *p. 121*				
	3x3-6	3x3-6	3x3-6	3x3-6	Squat Jump, *p. 122*	3x3-6	3x3-6		
		3x3-6	3x3-6	3x3-6	Double-Leg Slide Kick, *p. 123*		3x3-6	3x3-6	3x3-6
		3x3-6	3x3-6	3x3-6	Knee Tuck Jump, *p. 124*			3x3-6	3x3-6
		2x4-8	2x4-8	2x4-8	Split Jump, *p. 125*				
		2x6-12	2x6-12	2x6-12	Scissor Jump, *p. 126*				
					Depth Jump, *p. 127*				
Bounding	3x8-12	3x8-12	3x8-12	3x8-12	Prance, *p. 128*				
	2x8-12	2x8-12	2x8-12	2x8-12	Gallop, *p. 129*				
	3x8-12	3x8-12	3x8-12	3x8-12	Fast Skip, *p. 130*				
		3x3-6	3x3-6	3x3-6	Power Skip, *p. 130*			3x3-6	3x3-6
		2x8-12	2x8-12	2x8-12	Ankle Flip, *p. 131*				
				2x8-12	Bounding, *p. 132*				
				3x4-6	Lateral Bounding, *p. 133*				
Hopping	3x3-6	3x3-6	3x3-6	3x3-6	Double-Leg Hops, *p. 134*				
	3x3-6	3x3-6	3x3-6	3x3-6	Side Hops, *p. 135*				
	3x3-6	3x3-6	3x3-6	3x3-6	Single-Leg Pogo, *p. 136*				
				3x3-6	Single-Leg Slide Kick, *p. 137*				
				3x3-6	Single-Leg Hops, *p. 138*				
				3x3-6	Diagonal Hops, *p. 139*				
				2x3-6	Lateral Hops, *p. 140*				
Tosses/Throws	2x5	2x5	2x5	2x5	Shovel Toss, *p. 141*	2x5	2x5	2x5	
	2x5	2x5	2x5	2x5	Scoop Toss, *p. 142*	2x5	2x5	2x5	
	2x6	2x6	2x6	2x6	Twist Toss, *p. 143*	2x6	2x6	2x6	2x6
		2x5	2x5	2x5	Scoop Throw, *p. 144*		2x5	2x5	2x5
		2x6	2x6	2x6	Diagonal Throw, *p. 145*		2x6	2x6	2x6
		1x5	1x5	1x5	Kneeling Forward Throw, *p. 146*	2x5	2x5	2x5	2x5
				1x5	Standing Forward Throw, *p. 147*	2x5	2x5	2x5	2x5
					Stepping Forward Throw, *p. 148*	2x5	2x5	2x5	2x5
Push-Ups	2x5	2x5	2x5	2x5	Wall Push-Up, *p. 149*	2x5	2x5	2x5	2x5
	2x5	2x5			Drop Push-Up, *p. 150*				
		2x5	2x5	2x5	Kneeling Chest Pass, *p. 151*			2x5	2x5
					Chest Pass, *p. 152*				

	Exercise	Phase 1 (weeks 1–3)	Phase 2 (weeks 4–6)	Phase 3 (weeks 7–9)	Phase 4 (weeks 10–12)
COMPLEXES	Good Morning/Overhead Press/Overhead Squat, pp. 95, 109, 100	3x5-8	3x5-8	3x5-8	3x5-8
	Front Squat/Jerk, pp. 102, 118	5x2-4	5x2-4	5x2-4	
	Power Clean/Scoop Toss, pp. 117, 142	3x2-4	3x2-4	3x2-4	3x2-4
	Lunge/Split Jump, pp. 66, 125	2x4-8	2x4-8	2x4-8	
	Clean & Jerk, p. 118	4x1-3	4x1-3	4x1-3	4x1-3
	Front Squat & Jerk, pp. 102, 118	4x1-3	4x1-3	4x1-3	4x1-3
	Overhead Press/Overhead Squat, pp. 109, 100		3x5-8	3x5-8	3x5-8
	Clean & Front Squat & Jerk, pp. 116, 102, 118	4x1-3	4x1-3	4x1-3	4x1-3
COMBOS — Starts	Squared Step, p. 153	2x/leg	2x/leg	2x/leg	2x/leg
	Staggered Step, p. 153	2x/side	2x/side	2x/leg	2x/leg
	Open Step, p. 154				
	Crossover Step, p. 154				
	Drop Step, p. 155				
	Pivot Step, p. 155				
	Balanced Starts, p. 156	2x/side	2x/side	2x/side	2x/side
	Resisted Starts, p. 157	2x/side	2x/side	2x/side	2x/side
SPRINT TRAINING — Acceleration	"A" Walk, p. 158	2x20yds	2x20yds		
	"A" Skip, p. 158	2x20yds	2x20yds		
	Wall Drill, p. 160	2x6-10	2x6-10		
	"A" Run (Slide kick), p. 158	2x20yds	2x20yds		
SPRINT TRAINING — Speed	"B" Walk, p. 161	2x20yds	2x20yds		
	"B" Skip, p. 161	2x20yds	2x20yds		
	Cadence Fast Leg, p. 162	2x20yds	2x20yds		
	Sit Drill, p. 163	2x20yds	2x20yds		
AGILITY	Sway Drill, p. 164	1x6	1x6	1x6	
	Speed Weave, p. 166				
	Shuttle Run, p. 167				
	Power Weave, p. 168				4-6x
	3-Cone "L" Run, p. 169				
	Directional Drill, p. 170				4-6x

* phase 1 = weeks 1–3   phase 2 = weeks 4–6   phase 3 = weeks 7–9   phase 4 = weeks 10–12

FOOTBALL — line positions | EXERCISE | FOOTBALL — skill positions

MODE	*phase 1	phase 2	phase 3	phase 4	EXERCISE	*phase 1	phase 2	phase 3	phase 4
Jumping	3x8–12	3x8–12			Pogo, p. 121	3x8–12	3x8–12		
	3x3–6	3x3–6			Squat Jump, p. 122	3x3–6	3x3–6		
		3x3–6	3x3–6		Double-Leg Slide Kick, p. 123		3x3–6	3x3–6	
		3x3–6	3x3–6	3x3–6	Knee Tuck Jump, p. 124		3x3–6	3x3–6	3x3–6
		2x4–8	2x4–8	2x4–8	Split Jump, p. 125		2x4–8	2x4–8	2x4–8
		2x6–12	2x6–12	2x6–12	Scissor Jump, p. 126		2x6–12	2x6–12	2x6–12
					Depth Jump, p. 127				1x4–6
Bounding	3x8–12	3x8–12	3x8–12		Prance, p. 128	3x8–12	3x8–12	3x8–12	3x8–12
	2x8–12	2x8–12	2x8–12		Gallop, p. 129	2x8–12	2x8–12	2x8–12	2x8–12
	3x8–12	3x8–12	3x8–12		Fast Skip, p. 130	3x8–12	3x8–12	3x8–12	3x8–12
			3x3–6	3x3–6	Power Skip, p. 130			3x3–6	3x3–6
		2x8–12	3x8–12	3x8–12	Ankle Flip, p. 131		2x8–12	2x8–12	3x8–12
			2x8–12	2x8–12	Bounding, p. 132			2x8–12	2x8–12
	3x4–6	3x4–6	3x4–6	3x3–6	Lateral Bounding, p. 133				2x8–12
Hopping	3x3–6	3x3–6	3x3–6	3x3–6	Double-Leg Hops, p. 134		3x3–6	3x3–6	3x3–6
	3x3–6	3x3–6	3x3–6	3x3–6	Side Hops, p. 135		3x3–6	3x3–6	3x3–6
	3x3–6	3x3–6	3x3–6	3x3–6	Single-Leg Pogo, p. 136		3x3–6	3x3–6	3x3–6
				3x3–6	Single-Leg Slide Kick, p. 137				3x3–6
					Single-Leg Hops, p. 138				3x3–6
					Diagonal Hops, p. 139				3x3–6
					Lateral Hops, p. 140				3x3–6
Tosses/Throws	2x5	2x5	2x5		Shovel Toss, p. 141	2x5	2x5	2x5	
	2x5	2x5	2x5		Scoop Toss, p. 142	2x5	2x5	2x5	
	2x6	2x6	2x6		Twist Toss, p. 143	2x6	2x6	2x6	
			2x5	2x5	Scoop Throw, p. 144			2x5	2x5
			2x6	2x6	Diagonal Throw, p. 145			2x6	2x6
					Kneeling Forward Throw, p. 146	for Qb's only	1x5	1x5	2x5
					Standing Forward Throw, p. 147		1x5	1x5	2x5
					Stepping Forward Throw, p. 148		1x5	1x5	2x5
Push-Ups	2x5	2x5	2x5	2x5	Wall Push-Up, p. 149	2x5	2x5	2x5	2x5
					Drop Push-Up, p. 150				
		2x5	2x5	2x5	Kneeling Chest Pass, p. 151		2x5	2x5	2x5
		2x5	2x5	2x5	Chest Pass, p. 152		2x5	2x5	2x5

PLYOMETRICS

	Exercise (page refs)	Phase 1 (wks 1–3)	Phase 2 (wks 4–6)	Phase 3 (wks 7–9)	Phase 4 (wks 10–12)
COMPLEXES	Good Morning/Overhead Press/Overhead Squat, pp. 95, 109, 100	3x5–8	3x5–8	3x5–8	3x5–8
	Front Squat/Jerk, pp. 102, 118	5x2–4	5x2–4	5x2–4	5x2–4
	Power Clean/Scoop Toss, pp. 117, 142	3x2–4	3x2–4	3x2–4	3x2–4
	Lunge/Split Jump, pp. 66, 125	2x4–8	2x4–8	2x4–8	2x4–8
COMBOS	Clean & Jerk, p. 118		4x1–3	4x1–3	4x1–3
	Front Squat & Jerk, pp. 102, 118	4x1–3	4x1–3	4x1–3	4x1–3
	Overhead Press/Overhead Squat, pp. 109, 100	3x5–8	3x5–8	3x5–8	3x5–8
	Clean & Front Squat & Jerk, pp. 116, 102, 118	4x1–3	4x1–3	4x1–3	4x1–3
SPRINT TRAINING — Starts	Squared Step, p. 153	2x/leg	2x/leg	2x/leg	2x/leg
	Staggered Step, p. 153	2x/side	2x/side	2x/side	2x/side
	Open Step, p. 154	2x/side	2x/side	2x/side	2x/side
	Crossover Step, p. 154	2x/side	2x/side	2x/side	2x/side
	Drop Step, p. 155	2x/side	2x/side	2x/side	2x/side
	Pivot Step, p. 155			2x/side	2x/side
	Balanced Starts, p. 156		2x/side	2x/side	2x/side
	Resisted Starts, p. 157		2x/side	2x/side	2x/side
Acceleration	"A" Walk, p. 158	2x20yds	2x20yds	2x20yds	2x20yds
	"A" Skip, p. 158	2x20yds	2x20yds	2x20yds	2x20yds
	Wall Drill, p. 160	2x6–10	2x6–10	2x6–10	2x6–10
	"A" Run (Slide kick), p. 158	2x20yds	2x20yds	2x20yds	2x20yds
Speed	"B" Walk, p. 161		2x20yds	2x20yds	2x20yds
	"B" Skip, p. 161		2x20yds	2x20yds	2x20yds
	Cadence Fast Leg, p. 162		2x30yds	2x30yds	2x30yds
AGILITY	Sit Drill, p. 163	1x6	1x6	1x6	1x6
	Sway Drill, p. 164		1x6	1x6	1x6
	Speed Weave, p. 166	4–6x	4–6x	4–6x	4–6x
	Shuttle Run, p. 167	4–6x	4–6x	4–6x	4–6x
	Power Weave, p. 168		4–6x	4–6x	4–6x
	3-Cone "L" Run, p. 169		4–6x	4–6x	4–6x
	Directional Drill, p. 170		4–6x	4–6x	4–6x

*phase 1 = weeks 1–3   phase 2 = weeks 4–6   phase 3 = weeks 7–9   phase 4 = weeks 10–12

GYMNASTICS — EXERCISE — HOCKEY / LACROSSE

MODE — PLYOMETRICS

GYM *phase 1	GYM phase 2	GYM phase 3	GYM phase 4	EXERCISE	H/L *phase 1	H/L phase 2	H/L phase 3	H/L phase 4	MODE
3x8-12	3x8-12			Pogo, p. 121	3x8-12	3x8-12	3x8-12		Jumping
3x3-6	3x3-6	3x3-6		Squat Jump, p. 122	3x3-6	3x3-6	3x3-6		Jumping
	3x3-6	3x3-6	3x3-6	Double-Leg Slide Kick, p. 123		3x3-6	3x3-6	3x3-6	Jumping
	3x3-6	3x3-6	3x3-6	Knee Tuck Jump, p. 124		3x3-6	3x3-6	3x3-6	Jumping
	2x4-8	2x4-8	2x4-8	Split Jump, p. 125		2x4-8	2x4-8	2x4-8	Jumping
	2x6-12	2x6-12	2x6-12	Scissor Jump, p. 126		2x6-12	2x6-12	2x6-12	Jumping
		2x8-12	2x8-12	Depth Jump, p. 127			2x8-12	2x8-12	Jumping
3x8-12	3x8-12	3x8-12		Prance, p. 128	3x8-12	3x8-12	3x8-12		Bounding
	2x8-12	2x8-12	2x8-12	Gallop, p. 129					Bounding
3x3-6	3x3-6	3x3-6		Fast Skip, p. 130		3x3-6	3x3-6	3x3-6	Bounding
	3x3-6	3x3-6	3x3-6	Power Skip, p. 130		3x3-6	3x3-6	3x3-6	Bounding
	2x8-12	2x8-12	2x8-12	Ankle Flip, p. 131					Bounding
		2x8-12	2x8-12	Bounding, p. 132					Bounding
3x4-6	3x4-6	3x4-6		Lateral Bounding, p. 133	3x4-6	3x4-6	3x4-6		Bounding
3x3-6	3x3-6	3x3-6		Double-Leg Hops, p. 134	3x3-6	3x3-6	3x3-6		Hopping
	3x3-6	3x3-6	3x3-6	Side Hops, p. 135		3x3-6	3x3-6	3x3-6	Hopping
3x3-6	3x3-6	3x3-6		Single-Leg Pogo, p. 136		3x3-6	3x3-6	3x3-6	Hopping
		3x3-6	3x3-6	Single-Leg Slide Kick, p. 137				3x3-6	Hopping
		3x3-6	3x3-6	Single-Leg Hops, p. 138				3x3-6	Hopping
		3x3-6	3x3-6	Diagonal Hops, p. 139				3x3-6	Hopping
			2x3-6	Lateral Hops, p. 140				2x3-6	Hopping
2x5	2x5	2x5		Shovel Toss, p. 141	2x5	2x5	2x5		Tosses/Throws
2x5	2x5	2x5		Scoop Toss, p. 142	2x5	2x5	2x5		Tosses/Throws
2x6	2x6	2x6		Twist Toss, p. 143	2x6	2x6	2x6		Tosses/Throws
	2x5	2x5	2x5	Scoop Throw, p. 144		2x5	2x5	2x5	Tosses/Throws
	2x6	2x6	2x6	Diagonal Throw, p. 145		2x6	2x6	2x6	Tosses/Throws
	1x5	1x5		Kneeling Forward Throw, p. 146		1x5	1x5		Tosses/Throws
	1x5	1x5		Standing Forward Throw, p. 147		1x5	1x5		Tosses/Throws
		1x5		Stepping Forward Throw, p. 148			1x5		Tosses/Throws
2x5	2x5			Wall Push-Up, p. 149	2x5	2x5			Push-Ups
		2x5	2x5	Drop Push-Up, p. 150				2x5	Push-Ups
2x5	2x5	2x5		Kneeling Chest Pass, p. 151	2x5	2x5	2x5		Push-Ups
	2x5	2x5	2x5	Chest Pass, p. 152			2x5	2x5	Push-Ups

	Phase 1 (weeks 1–3)	Phase 2 (weeks 4–6)	Phase 3 (weeks 7–9)	Phase 4 (weeks 10–12)
COMPLEXES				
Good Morning/Overhead Press/Overhead Squat, pp. 95, 109, 100	3x5-8	3x5-8	3x5-8	3x5-8
Front Squat/Jerk, pp. 102, 118	5x2-4	5x2-4	5x2-4	5x2-4
Power Clean/Scoop Toss, pp. 117, 142	3x2-4	3x2-4	3x2-4	3x2-4
Lunge/Split Jump, pp. 66, 125	2x4-8	2x4-8	2x4-8	2x4-8
COMBOS				
Clean & Jerk, p. 118	4x1-3	4x1-3	4x1-3	4x1-3
Front Squat & Jerk, pp. 102, 118	4x1-3	4x1-3	4x1-3	4x1-3
Overhead Press/Overhead Squat, pp. 109, 100			3x5-8	3x5-8
Clean & Front Squat & Jerk, pp. 116, 102, 118	4x1-3	4x1-3	4x1-3	4x1-3
SPRINT TRAINING — Starts				
Squared Step, p. 153	2x/side	2x/side	2x/leg	2x/leg
Staggered Step, p. 153	2x/side	2x/side	2x/side	2x/side
Open Step, p. 154			2x/side	2x/side
Crossover Step, p. 154			2x/side	2x/side
Drop Step, p. 155			2x/side	2x/side
Pivot Step, p. 155			2x/side	2x/side
Balanced Starts, p. 156	2x/side	2x/side	2x/side	2x/side
Resisted Starts, p. 157	2x/side	2x/side	2x/side	2x/side
SPRINT TRAINING — Acceleration				
"A" Walk, p. 158	2x20yds	2x20yds	2x20yds	2x20yds
"A" Skip, p. 158	2x20yds	2x20yds	2x20yds	2x20yds
Wall Drill, p. 160	2x6-10	2x6-10	2x6-10	2x6-10
"A" Run (Slide kick), p. 158	2x20yds	2x20yds	2x20yds	2x20yds
SPRINT TRAINING — Speed				
"B" Walk, p. 161			2x20yds	2x20yds
"B" Skip, p. 161			2x20yds	2x20yds
Cadence Fast Leg, p. 162		2x20yds	2x20yds	2x20yds
AGILITY				
Sit Drill, p. 163	1x6	1x6	1x6	
Sway Drill, p. 164			1x6	1x6
Speed Weave, p. 166			4-6x	4-6x
Shuttle Run, p. 167	4-6x	4-6x	4-6x	4-6x
Power Weave, p. 168			4-6x	4-6x
3-Cone "L" Run, p. 169			4-6x	4-6x
Directional Drill, p. 170			4-6x	4-6x

* phase 1 = weeks 1–3   phase 2 = weeks 4–6   phase 3 = weeks 7–9   phase 4 = weeks 10–12

PLYOMETRICS

MODE	EXERCISE	RACQUET SPORTS *phase 1	phase 2	phase 3	phase 4	RUGBY *phase 1	phase 2	phase 3	phase 4
Jumping	Pogo, *p. 121*	3x8-12	3x8-12	3x8-12		3x8-12	3x8-12	3x8-12	
Jumping	Squat Jump, *p. 122*	3x3-6	3x3-6	3x3-6		3x3-6	3x3-6	3x3-6	
Jumping	Double-Leg Slide Kick, *p. 123*		3x3-6	3x3-6	3x3-6		3x3-6	3x3-6	3x3-6
Jumping	Knee Tuck Jump, *p. 124*		3x3-6	3x3-6	3x3-6		3x3-6	3x3-6	3x3-6
Jumping	Split Jump, *p. 125*		2x4-8	2x4-8	2x4-8		2x4-8	2x4-8	2x4-8
Jumping	Scissor Jump, *p. 126*		2x6-12	2x6-12	2x6-12		2x6-12	2x6-12	2x6-12
Jumping	Depth Jump, *p. 127*				1x4-6				1x4-6
Bounding	Prance, *p. 128*	3x8-12	3x8-12	3x8-12		3x8-12	3x8-12	3x8-12	
Bounding	Gallop, *p. 129*	2x8-12	2x8-12	2x8-12		2x8-12	2x8-12	2x8-12	
Bounding	Fast Skip, *p. 130*	3x8-12	3x8-12	3x8-12		3x8-12	3x8-12	3x8-12	
Bounding	Power Skip, *p. 130*			3x3-6	3x3-6			3x3-6	3x3-6
Bounding	Ankle Flip, *p. 131*		2x8-12	3x8-12	3x8-12		2x8-12	3x8-12	3x8-12
Bounding	Bounding, *p. 132*			2x8-12	2x8-12			2x8-12	2x8-12
Bounding	Lateral Bounding, *p. 133*			2x8-12	2x8-12			2x8-12	2x8-12
Hopping	Double-Leg Hops, *p. 134*	3x3-6	3x3-6	3x3-6		3x3-6	3x3-6	3x3-6	
Hopping	Side Hops, *p. 135*	3x3-6	3x3-6	3x3-6		3x3-6	3x3-6	3x3-6	
Hopping	Single-Leg Pogo, *p. 136*	3x3-6	3x3-6	3x3-6		3x3-6	3x3-6	3x3-6	
Hopping	Single-Leg Slide Kick, *p. 137*				3x3-6				3x3-6
Hopping	Single-Leg Hops, *p. 138*				3x3-6				3x3-6
Hopping	Diagonal Hops, *p. 139*				3x3-6				3x3-6
Hopping	Lateral Hops, *p. 140*				3x3-6				3x3-6
Tosses/Throws	Shovel Toss, *p. 141*	2x5	2x5			2x5	2x5		
Tosses/Throws	Scoop Toss, *p. 142*	2x5	2x5			2x5	2x5		
Tosses/Throws	Twist Toss, *p. 143*	2x6	2x6			2x6	2x6		
Tosses/Throws	Scoop Throw, *p. 144*			2x5	2x5			2x5	2x5
Tosses/Throws	Diagonal Throw, *p. 145*			2x6	2x6			2x6	2x6
Tosses/Throws	Kneeling Forward Throw, *p. 146*			1x5	1x5			1x5	1x5
Tosses/Throws	Standing Forward Throw, *p. 147*			1x5	1x5			1x5	1x5
Tosses/Throws	Stepping Forward Throw, *p. 148*			1x5	1x5			1x5	1x5
Push-Ups	Wall Push-Up, *p. 149*	2x5	2x5			2x5	2x5		
Push-Ups	Drop Push-Up, *p. 150*			2x5	2x5			2x5	2x5
Push-Ups	Kneeling Chest Pass, *p. 151*	2x5	2x5			2x5	2x5		
Push-Ups	Chest Pass, *p. 152*			2x5	2x5			2x5	2x5

Category	Exercise							
COMPLEXES	Good Morning/Overhead Press/ Overhead Squat, pp. 95, 109, 100	3x5-8	3x5-8	3x5-8	3x5-8	3x5-8	3x5-8	3x5-8
	Front Squat/Jerk, pp. 102, 118	5x2-4				5x2-4		
	Power Clean/Scoop Toss, pp. 117, 142	3x2-4	3x2-4	3x2-4	3x2-4	3x2-4	3x2-4	3x2-4
	Lunge/Split Jump, pp. 66, 125	2x4-8	2x4-8			2x4-8	2x4-8	
COMBOS	Clean & Jerk, p. 118		4x1-3	4x1-3	4x1-3	4x1-3		
	Front Squat & Jerk, pp. 102, 118	4x1-3	4x1-3	4x1-3	4x1-3	4x1-3	4x1-3	
	Overhead Press/Overhead Squat, pp. 109, 100		3x5-8	3x5-8	3x5-8	3x5-8	3x5-8	3x5-8
	Clean & Front Squat & Jerk, pp. 116, 102, 118	4x1-3	4x1-3	4x1-3	4x1-3	4x1-3	4x1-3	4x1-3
SPRINT TRAINING (Starts)	Squared Step, p. 153	2x/leg	2x/leg	2x/leg	2x/leg	2x/leg	2x/leg	2x/leg
	Staggered Step, p. 153	2x/side	2x/side	2x/side	2x/side	2x/side	2x/side	2x/side
	Open Step, p. 154	2x/side	2x/side	2x/side	2x/side	2x/side	2x/side	2x/side
	Crossover Step, p. 154				2x/side			2x/side
	Drop Step, p. 155	2x/side	2x/side	2x/side	2x/side	2x/side	2x/side	2x/side
	Pivot Step, p. 155	2x/side	2x/side					
	Balanced Starts, p. 156	2x/side	2x/side	2x/side	2x/side	2x/side	2x/side	2x/side
	Resisted Starts, p. 157	2x/side	2x/side	2x/side	2x/side	2x/side	2x/side	2x/side
(Acceleration)	"A" Walk, p. 158	2x20yds	2x20yds	2x20yds	2x20yds	2x20yds	2x20yds	2x20yds
	"A" Skip, p. 158	2x20yds	2x20yds	2x20yds	2x20yds	2x20yds	2x20yds	2x20yds
	Wall Drill, p. 160	2x6-10	2x6-10	2x6-10	2x6-10	2x6-10	2x6-10	2x6-10
	"A" Run (Slide kick), p. 158	2x20yds	2x20yds	2x20yds	2x20yds	2x20yds	2x20yds	2x20yds
(Speed)	"B" Walk, p. 161					2x20yds	2x20yds	2x20yds
	"B" Skip, p. 161					2x20yds	2x20yds	2x20yds
	Cadence Fast Leg, p. 162					2x30yds	2x30yds	2x30yds
AGILITY	Sit Drill, p. 163	1x6	1x6	1x6	1x6	1x6		
	Sway Drill, p. 164	1x6	1x6	1x6	1x6	1x6	1x6	
	Speed Weave, p. 166	4-6x	4-6x	4-6x	4-6x	4-6x	4-6x	4-6x
	Shuttle Run, p. 167	4-6x	4-6x	4-6x	4-6x	4-6x	4-6x	4-6x
	Power Weave, p. 168			4-6x	4-6x	4-6x	4-6x	4-6x
	3-Cone "L" Run, p. 169	4-6x	4-6x	4-6x	4-6x	4-6x	4-6x	4-6x
	Directional Drill, p. 170	4-6x	4-6x	4-6x	4-6x	4-6x	4-6x	4-6x

PLYOMETRICS

MODE	EXERCISE	SKIING–alpine				SKIING–nordic			
		*phase 1	phase 2	phase 3	phase 4	*phase 1	phase 2	phase 3	phase 4
Jumping	Pogo, p. 121	3x8–12	3x8–12			3x8–12	3x8–12		
	Squat Jump, p. 122	3x3–6	3x3–6			3x3–6	3x3–6		
	Double-Leg Slide Kick, p. 123		3x3–6	3x3–6	3x3–6		3x3–6	3x3–6	3x3–6
	Knee Tuck Jump, p. 124		2x4–8	2x4–8	2x4–8		2x4–8	2x4–8	2x4–8
	Split Jump, p. 125		2x6–12	2x6–12	2x6–12		2x6–12	2x6–12	2x6–12
	Scissor Jump, p. 126								
	Depth Jump, p. 127				1x4–6				1x4–6
Bounding	Prance, p. 128	3x8–12	3x8–12	3x8–12		3x8–12	3x8–12	3x8–12	
	Gallop, p. 129	2x8–12	2x8–12	2x8–12		2x8–12	2x8–12	2x8–12	
	Fast Skip, p. 130	3x8–12	3x8–12	3x8–12		3x8–12	3x8–12	3x8–12	
	Power Skip, p. 130		3x3–6	3x3–6			3x3–6	3x3–6	
	Ankle Flip, p. 131		2x8–12	3x8–12	3x8–12		2x8–12	3x8–12	3x8–12
	Bounding, p. 132		2x8–12	2x8–12	2x8–12		2x8–12	2x8–12	2x8–12
	Lateral Bounding, p. 133	3x4–6	3x4–6	3x4–6		3x4–6	3x4–6	3x4–6	
Hopping	Double-Leg Hops, p. 134		3x3–6	3x3–6	3x3–6				
	Side Hops, p. 135		3x3–6	3x3–6	3x3–6				
	Single-Leg Pogo, p. 136		3x3–6	3x3–6	3x3–6				
	Single-Leg Slide Kick, p. 137			3x3–6	3x8–12				
	Single-Leg Hops, p. 138				3x3–6				
	Diagonal Hops, p. 139				3x3–6				
	Lateral Hops, p. 140				2x3–6				
Tosses/Throws	Shovel Toss, p. 141	2x5	2x5			2x5	2x5		
	Scoop Toss, p. 142	2x5	2x5			2x5	2x5		
	Twist Toss, p. 143	2x6	2x6			2x6	2x6		
	Scoop Throw, p. 144	2x5	2x5	2x5	2x5	2x5	2x5	2x5	2x5
	Diagonal Throw, p. 145		2x6	2x6	2x6		2x6	2x6	2x6
	Kneeling Forward Throw, p. 146	1x5	1x5	1x5	1x5	1x5	1x5	1x5	1x5
	Standing Forward Throw, p. 147	1x5	1x5	1x5	1x5	1x5	1x5	1x5	1x5
	Stepping Forward Throw, p. 148				1x5				1x5
Push-Ups	Wall Push-Up, p. 149								
	Drop Push-Up, p. 150								
	Kneeling Chest Pass, p. 151								
	Chest Pass, p. 152								

Category	Exercise (page ref)	Phase 1 (wk 1–3)	Phase 2 (wk 4–6)	Phase 3 (wk 7–9)	Phase 4 (wk 10–12)
COMPLEXES	Good Morning/Overhead Press/Overhead Squat, pp. 95, 109, 100	3x5-8	3x5-8	3x5-8	3x5-8
	Front Squat/Jerk, pp. 102, 118	5x2-4	5x2-4	5x2-4	5x2-4
	Power Clean/Scoop Toss, pp. 117, 142	3x2-4	3x2-4	3x2-4	3x2-4
	Lunge/Split Jump, pp. 66, 125	2x4-8	2x4-8	2x4-8	2x4-8
	Clean & Jerk, p. 118	4x1-3	4x1-3	4x1-3	4x1-3
	Front Squat & Jerk, pp. 102, 118	4x1-3	4x1-3	4x1-3	4x1-3
	Overhead Press/Overhead Squat, pp. 109, 100			3x5-8	3x5-8
	Clean & Front Squat & Jerk, pp. 116, 102, 118	4x1-3	4x1-3	4x1-3	4x1-3
COMBOS (Starts)	Squared Step, p. 153	2x/leg	2x/leg	2x/leg	2x/leg
	Staggered Step, p. 153	2x/side	2x/side	2x/side	2x/side
	Open Step, p. 154		2x/side	2x/side	2x/side
	Crossover Step, p. 154				
	Drop Step, p. 155				
	Pivot Step, p. 155	2x/side		2x/side	2x/side
	Balanced Starts, p. 156	2x/side	2x/side	2x/side	2x/side
	Resisted Starts, p. 157	2x/side	2x/side	2x/side	2x/side
SPRINT TRAINING (Acceleration)	"A" Walk, p. 158	2x20yds	2x20yds	2x20yds	2x20yds
	"A" Skip, p. 158	2x20yds	2x20yds	2x20yds	2x20yds
	Wall Drill, p. 160	2x6-10	2x6-10	2x6-10	2x6-10
	"A" Run (Slide kick), p. 158	2x20yds	2x20yds	2x20yds	2x20yds
(Speed)	"B" Walk, p. 161				
	"B" Skip, p. 161				
	Cadence Fast Leg, p. 162			2x/leg	2x/leg
AGILITY	Sit Drill, p. 163	1x6			
	Sway Drill, p. 164	1x6	1x6	1x6	1x6
	Speed Weave, p. 166	4-6x	4-6x	4-6x	4-6x
	Shuttle Run, p. 167		4-6x	4-6x	4-6x
	Power Weave, p. 168	4-6x	4-6x	4-6x	4-6x
	3-Cone "L" Run, p. 169	4-6x	4-6x	4-6x	4-6x
	Directional Drill, p. 170	4-6x	4-6x	4-6x	4-6x

* phase 1 = weeks 1–3   phase 2 = weeks 4–6   phase 3 = weeks 7–9   phase 4 = weeks 10–12

MODE	SOCCER				EXERCISE	SWIMMING			
	*phase 1	phase 2	phase 3	phase 4		*phase 1	phase 2	phase 3	phase 4
Jumping	3x8-12	3x8-12			Pogo, p. 121	3x8-12	3x8-12		
	3x3-6	3x3-6	3x3-6		Squat Jump, p. 122	3x3-6	3x3-6		
	3x8-12	3x8-12	3x8-12	3x3-6	Double-Leg Slide Kick, p. 123				
		3x3-6	3x3-6	3x3-6	Knee Tuck Jump, p. 124		3x3-6	3x3-6	3x3-6
		2x4-8	2x4-8	2x4-8	Split Jump, p. 125		2x4-8	2x4-8	2x4-8
		2x6-12	2x6-12	2x6-12	Scissor Jump, p. 126		2x6-12	2x6-12	2x6-12
				1x4-6	Depth Jump, p. 127				1x4-6
Bounding	3x8-12	3x8-12	3x8-12		Prance, p. 128				
	2x8-12	2x8-12	2x8-12		Gallop, p. 129				
	3x8-12	3x8-12	3x8-12		Fast Skip, p. 130				
		2x8-12	3x3-6	3x3-6	Power Skip, p. 130	3x3-6	3x3-6	3x3-6	3x3-6
			3x8-12	3x8-12	Ankle Flip, p. 131				
		2x8-12	2x8-12	2x8-12	Bounding, p. 132				
	3x4-6	3x4-6	3x4-6	2x3-6	Lateral Bounding, p. 133				
Hopping		3x3-6	3x3-6	3x3-6	Double-Leg Hops, p. 134		3x3-6	3x3-6	3x3-6
		3x3-6	3x3-6	3x3-6	Side Hops, p. 135				
			3x3-6	3x3-6	Single-Leg Pogo, p. 136			3x3-6	3x3-6
				3x3-6	Single-Leg Slide Kick, p. 137				
				3x3-6	Single-Leg Hops, p. 138				
				3x3-6	Diagonal Hops, p. 139				
				2x3-6	Lateral Hops, p. 140				
Tosses/Throws	2x5	2x5	2x5		Shovel Toss, p. 141	2x5	2x5	2x5	
	2x5	2x5	2x5		Scoop Toss, p. 142	2x5	2x5	2x5	
	2x6	2x6	2x6		Twist Toss, p. 143	2x6	2x6	2x6	
		2x5	2x5	2x5	Scoop Throw, p. 144		2x5	2x5	2x5
			2x6	2x6	Diagonal Throw, p. 145		2x6	2x6	2x6
		1x5	1x5	1x5	Kneeling Forward Throw, p. 146		1x5	1x5	2x5
		1x5	1x5	1x5	Standing Forward Throw, p. 147		1x5	1x5	2x5
			1x5	1x5	Stepping Forward Throw, p. 148		1x5	1x5	2x5
Push-Ups	2x5	2x5	2x5		Wall Push-Up, p. 149				
				2x5	Drop Push-Up, p. 150				
	2x5	2x5	2x5		Kneeling Chest Pass, p. 151				
				2x5	Chest Pass, p. 152				

PLYOMETRICS

Category	Exercise	Phase 1 (wks 1–3)	Phase 2 (wks 4–6)	Phase 3 (wks 7–9)	Phase 4 (wks 10–12)
COMPLEXES	Good Morning/Overhead Press/Overhead Squat, pp. 95, 109, 100	3x5-8	3x5-8	3x5-8	3x5-8
	Front Squat/Jerk, pp. 102, 118	5x2-4	5x2-4	5x2-4	5x2-4
	Power Clean/Scoop Toss, pp. 117, 142	3x2-4	3x2-4	3x2-4	3x2-4
	Lunge/Split Jump, pp. 66, 125	2x4-8	2x4-8	2x4-8	2x4-8
COMBOS	Clean & Jerk, p. 118	4x1-3	4x1-3	4x1-3	4x1-3
	Front Squat & Jerk, pp. 102, 118	4x1-3	4x1-3	4x1-3	4x1-3
	Overhead Press/Overhead Squat, pp. 109, 100	3x5-8	3x5-8	3x5-8	3x5-8
	Clean & Front Squat & Jerk, pp. 116, 102, 118	4x1-3	4x1-3	4x1-3	4x1-3
SPRINT TRAINING — *Starts*	Squared Step, p. 153	2x/leg	2x/leg	2x/leg	2x/leg
	Staggered Step, p. 153	2x/side	2x/side	2x/side	2x/side
	Open Step, p. 154	2x/side	2x/side		
	Crossover Step, p. 154	2x/side	2x/side		
	Drop Step, p. 155	2x/side	2x/side		
	Pivot Step, p. 155	2x/side	2x/side		
	Balanced Starts, p. 156	2x/side	2x/side	2x/side	2x/side
	Resisted Starts, p. 157	2x/side	2x/side	2x/side	2x/side
Acceleration	"A" Walk, p. 158	2x20yds	2x20yds	2x20yds	2x20yds
	"A" Skip, p. 158	2x20yds	2x20yds	2x20yds	2x20yds
	Wall Drill, p. 160	2x6-10	2x6-10	2x6-10	2x6-10
	"A" Run (Slide kick), p. 158	2x20yds	2x20yds	2x20yds	2x20yds
Speed	"B" Walk, p. 161	2x20yds	2x20yds	2x20yds	2x20yds
	"B" Skip, p. 161	2x20yds	2x20yds	2x20yds	2x20yds
	Cadence Fast Leg, p. 162	2x20yds	2x20yds	2x20yds	2x20yds
AGILITY	Sit Drill, p. 163	1x6	1x6		
	Sway Drill, p. 164	1x6	1x6		
	Speed Weave, p. 166	4-6x	4-6x		
	Shuttle Run, p. 167		4-6x		
	Power Weave, p. 168	4-6x	4-6x		
	3-Cone "L" Run, p. 169	4-6x	4-6x		
	Directional Drill, p. 170	4-6x	4-6x		

* phase 1 = weeks 1–3 phase 2 = weeks 4–6 phase 3 = weeks 7–9 phase 4 = weeks 10–12

MODE (PLYOMETRICS)	TRACK & FIELD—distances *phase 1	phase 2	phase 3	phase 4	EXERCISE	TRACK & FIELD—sprints & jumps *phase 1	phase 2	phase 3	phase 4
Jumping	3x8–12	3x8–12			Pogo, *p. 121*	3x8–12	3x8–12		
	3x3–6	3x3–6			Squat Jump, *p. 122*	3x3–6	3x3–6		
		3x3–6			Double-Leg Slide Kick, *p. 123*	3x3–6	3x3–6		
		3x3–6	3x3–6	3x3–6	Knee Tuck Jump, *p. 124*		3x3–6	3x3–6	3x3–6
		2x4–8	2x4–8	2x4–8	Split Jump, *p. 125*		2x4–8	2x4–8	
			2x6–12	2x6–12	Scissor Jump, *p. 126*		2x6–12	2x6–12	2x6–12
					Depth Jump, *p. 127*				1x4–6
Bounding	3x8–12	3x8–12	3x8–12	3x8–12	Prance, *p. 128*	3x8–12	3x8–12	3x8–12	
	2x8–12	2x8–12	2x8–12	2x8–12	Gallop, *p. 129*	2x8–12	3x8–12	3x8–12	
	2x8–12	3x8–12	3x8–12	3x8–12	Fast Skip, *p. 130*	3x8–12	3x8–12	3x8–12	
			3x3–6	3x3–6	Power Skip, *p. 130*		3x3–6	3x3–6	3x3–6
		2x8–12	3x8–12	3x8–12	Ankle Flip, *p. 131*		2x8–12	3x8–12	3x8–12
				2x8–12	Bounding, *p. 132*			2x8–12	2x8–12
					Lateral Bounding, *p. 133*				
Hopping		3x3–6	3x3–6		Double-Leg Hops, *p. 134*			3x3–6	3x3–6
		3x3–6	3x3–6		Side Hops, *p. 135*			3x3–6	3x3–6
			3x3–6	3x3–6	Single-Leg Pogo, *p. 136*			3x3–6	3x3–6
				3x3–6	Single-Leg Slide Kick, *p. 137*			3x3–6	3x3–6
				3x3–6	Single-Leg Hops, *p. 138*			3x3–6	3x3–6
				3x3–6	Diagonal Hops, *p. 139*				3x3–6
				3x3–6	Lateral Hops, *p. 140*				
Tosses/Throws					Shovel Toss, *p. 141*	2x5	2x5	2x5	
		1x5	1x5	1x5	Scoop Toss, *p. 142*	2x5	2x5	2x5	
					Twist Toss, *p. 143*	2x6	2x6	2x6	
					Scoop Throw, *p. 144*			2x5	2x5
					Diagonal Throw, *p. 145*			2x6	2x6
			1x5	1x5	Kneeling Forward Throw, *p. 146*		1x5	1x5	2x5
			1x5	1x5	Standing Forward Throw, *p. 147*		1x5	1x5	2x5
			1x5	1x5	Stepping Forward Throw, *p. 148*				
Push-Ups	2x5	2x5	2x5	2x5	Wall Push-Up, *p. 149*	2x5	2x5		
					Drop Push-Up, *p. 150*			2x5	2x5
					Kneeling Chest Pass, *p. 151*	2x5	2x5		
					Chest Pass, *p. 152*			2x5	2x5

Training Program Chart (values are mirrored on both sides of the exercise list; shown once below)

Exercise	phase 1	phase 2	phase 3	phase 4
COMPLEXES				
Good Morning/Overhead Press/Overhead Squat, pp. 95, 109, 100	3x5-8	3x5-8	3x5-8	3x5-8
Front Squat/Jerk, pp. 102, 118	5x2-4	5x2-4	5x2-4	5x2-4
Power Clean/Scoop Toss, pp. 117, 142	3x2-4	3x2-4	3x2-4	3x2-4
Lunge/Split Jump, pp. 66, 125	2x4-8	2x4-8	2x4-8	2x4-8
COMBOS				
Clean & Jerk, p. 118		4x1-3	4x1-3	4x1-3
Front Squat & Jerk, pp. 102, 118		4x1-3	4x1-3	4x1-3
Overhead Press/Overhead Squat, pp. 109, 100		3x5-8	3x5-8	3x5-8
Clean & Front Squat & Jerk, pp. 116, 102, 118		4x1-3	4x1-3	4x1-3
Squared Step, p. 153	2x/side	2x/side	2x/leg	2x/leg
Staggered Step, p. 153	2x/side	2x/side	2x/side	2x/side
Open Step, p. 154	2x/side	2x/side	2x/side	2x/side
Crossover Step, p. 154			2x/side	2x/side
Drop Step, p. 155			2x/side	2x/side
Pivot Step, p. 155			2x/side	2x/side
Balanced Starts, p. 156	2x/side	2x/side	2x/side	2x/side
Resisted Starts, p. 157		2x/side	2x/side	2x/side
SPRINT TRAINING				
"A" Walk, p. 158	2x20yds	2x20yds	2x20yds	2x20yds
"A" Skip, p. 158	2x20yds	2x20yds	2x20yds	2x20yds
Wall Drill, p. 160	2x6-10	2x6-10	2x6-10	2x6-10
"A" Run (Slide kick), p. 158	2x20yds	2x20yds	2x20yds	2x20yds
"B" Walk, p. 161	2x20yds	2x20yds	2x20yds	2x20yds
"B" Skip, p. 161	2x20yds	2x20yds	2x20yds	2x20yds
Cadence Fast Leg, p. 162	2x30yds	2x30yds	2x30yds	2x30yds
AGILITY				
Sit Drill, p. 163	1x6	1x6	1x6	1x6
Sway Drill, p. 164	4-6x	4-6x	4-6x	4-6x
Speed Weave, p. 166				
Shuttle Run, p. 167				
Power Weave, p. 168				
3-Cone "L" Run, p. 169				
Directional Drill, p. 170				

Row-group labels (within Sprint Training): Starts · Acceleration · Speed

* phase 1 = weeks 1–3   phase 2 = weeks 4–6   phase 3 = weeks 7–9   phase 4 = weeks 10–12

PLYOMETRICS

MODE		TRACK & FIELD–throws				EXERCISE	VOLLEYBALL			
		*phase 1	phase 2	phase 3	phase 4		*phase 1	phase 2	phase 3	phase 4
Jumping		3x8-12	3x8-12			Pogo, p. 121	3x8-12	3x8-12	3x8-12	
		3x3-6	3x3-6	3x3-6	3x3-6	Squat Jump, p. 122	3x3-6	3x3-6	3x3-6	
			3x3-6	3x3-6	3x3-6	Double-Leg Slide Kick, p. 123		3x3-6	3x3-6	3x3-6
		3x3-6	3x3-6	3x3-6	3x3-6	Knee Tuck Jump, p. 124		3x3-6	3x3-6	3x3-6
			2x4-8	2x4-8	2x4-8	Split Jump, p. 125		2x4-8	2x4-8	2x4-8
				2x6-12	2x6-12	Scissor Jump, p. 126			2x6-12	2x6-12
						Depth Jump, p. 127				1x4-6
Bounding		3x8-12	3x8-12	3x8-12	3x8-12	Prance, p. 128	3x8-12	3x8-12	3x8-12	
		2x8-12	2x8-12	2x8-12	2x8-12	Gallop, p. 129	2x8-12	2x8-12	2x8-12	
		3x8-12	3x8-12	3x8-12	3x8-12	Fast Skip, p. 130	3x8-12	3x8-12	3x8-12	
				3x3-6	3x3-6	Power Skip, p. 130			3x3-6	3x3-6
		2x8-12	2x8-12	3x8-12	3x8-12	Ankle Flip, p. 131	2x8-12	2x8-12	3x8-12	3x8-12
					2x8-12	Bounding, p. 132				
					3x4-6	Lateral Bounding, p. 133				3x4-6
Hopping		3x4-6	3x4-6	3x4-6	3x4-6	Double-Leg Hops, p. 134	3x4-6	3x4-6	3x4-6	3x4-6
			3x3-6	3x3-6	3x3-6	Side Hops, p. 135		3x3-6	3x3-6	3x3-6
			3x3-6	3x3-6	3x3-6	Single-Leg Pogo, p. 136		3x3-6	3x3-6	3x3-6
				3x3-6	3x3-6	Single-Leg Slide Kick, p. 137			3x3-6	3x3-6
						Single-Leg Hops, p. 138				
						Diagonal Hops, p. 139				
					3x4-6	Lateral Hops, p. 140				3x4-6
Tosses/Throws		2x5	3x6-8	3x6-8	3x6-8	Shovel Toss, p. 141	2x5	2x5	2x5	
		2x5	3x6-8	3x6-8	3x6-8	Scoop Toss, p. 142	2x5	2x5	2x5	
		2x5	3x6-8	3x6-8	3x6-8	Twist Toss, p. 143	2x6	2x6	2x6	
		2x5	3x6-8	3x6-8	3x6-8	Scoop Throw, p. 144		2x5	2x5	2x5
		2x5	3x6-8	3x6-8	3x6-8	Diagonal Throw, p. 145		2x6	2x6	2x6
		2x5	3x6-8 *(for javelin only)*	3x6-8	3x6-8	Kneeling Forward Throw, p. 146	2x5	2x5	2x5	2x5
		2x5	3x6-8	3x6-8	3x6-8	Standing Forward Throw, p. 147	2x5	2x5	2x5	2x5
		2x5	3x6-8	3x6-8	3x6-8	Stepping Forward Throw, p. 148	2x5	2x5	2x5	2x5
Push-Ups		2x5	2x5	2x5	2x5	Wall Push-Up, p. 149	2x5	2x5		
		2x5	2x5	2x5	2x5	Drop Push-Up, p. 150				
						Kneeling Chest Pass, p. 151	2x5	2x5	2x5	2x5
						Chest Pass, p. 152	2x5	2x5	2x5	2x5

The following program chart is printed sideways on the page. Exercise names (with page references) run down the center; training volumes (sets × reps, distances, or repetitions) are listed for each training phase. Where a cell is blank, the exercise is not prescribed for that phase.

Category	Exercise	Col 1	Col 2	Col 3	Col 4	Col 5	Col 6	Col 7	Col 8
COMPLEXES	Good Morning/Overhead Press/Overhead Squat, pp. 95, 109, 100	3x5-8	3x5-8	3x5-8	3x5-8	3x5-8	3x5-8	3x5-8	3x5-8
	Front Squat/Jerk, pp. 102, 118	5x2-4	5x2-4	5x2-4		5x2-4		5x2-4	5x2-4
	Power Clean/Scoop Toss, pp. 117, 142	3x2-4	3x2-4	3x2-4	3x2-4	3x2-4	3x2-4	3x2-4	3x2-4
	Lunge/Split Jump, pp. 66, 125	2x4-8	2x4-8		2x4-8	2x4-8	2x4-8	2x4-8	
COMBOS	Clean & Jerk, p. 118	4x1-3	4x1-3		4x1-3	4x1-3		4x1-3	4x1-3
	Front Squat & Jerk, pp. 102, 118	4x1-3	4x1-3		4x1-3	4x1-3		4x1-3	4x1-3
	Overhead Press/Overhead Squat, pp. 109, 100	3x5-8	3x5-8	3x5-8	3x5-8	3x5-8	3x5-8	3x5-8	3x5-8
	Clean & Front Squat & Jerk, pp. 116, 102, 118	4x1-3	4x1-3		4x1-3	4x1-3	4x1-3	4x1-3	4x1-3
SPRINT TRAINING — Starts	Squared Step, p. 153	2x/leg	2x/leg			2x/leg	2x/leg	2x/leg	2x/leg
	Staggered Step, p. 153	2x/side	2x/side			2x/side	2x/side	2x/side	2x/side
	Open Step, p. 154	2x/side	2x/side			2x/side	2x/side	2x/side	2x/side
	Crossover Step, p. 154						2x/side	2x/side	2x/side
	Drop Step, p. 155	2x/side	2x/side			2x/side	2x/side	2x/side	2x/side
	Pivot Step, p. 155	2x/side	2x/side					2x/side	2x/side
	Balanced Starts, p. 156	2x/side	2x/side			2x/side	2x/side	2x/side	2x/side
	Resisted Starts, p. 157	2x/side	2x/side			2x/side	2x/side	2x/side	2x/side
Acceleration	"A" Walk, p. 158	2x20yds	2x20yds			2x20yds	2x20yds	2x20yds	2x20yds
	"A" Skip, p. 158	2x20yds	2x20yds			2x20yds	2x20yds	2x20yds	2x20yds
	Wall Drill, p. 160	2x6-10	2x6-10			2x6-10	2x6-10	2x6-10	2x6-10
	"A" Run (Slide kick), p. 158	2x20yds	2x20yds			2x20yds	2x20yds	2x20yds	2x20yds
Speed	"B" Walk, p. 161								
	"B" Skip, p. 161								
	Cadence Fast Leg, p. 162								
AGILITY	Sit Drill, p. 163	1x6				1x6			
	Sway Drill, p. 164	1x6	1x6			1x6	1x6	1x6	1x6
	Speed Weave, p. 166	4-6x	4-6x			4-6x	4-6x		
	Shuttle Run, p. 167					4-6x	4-6x	4-6x	4-6x
	Power Weave, p. 168								4-6x
	3-Cone "L" Run, p. 169	4-6x			4-6x		4-6x	4-6x	4-6x
	Directional Drill, p. 170						4-6x	4-6x	4-6x

* phase 1 = weeks 1–3   phase 2 = weeks 4–6   phase 3 = weeks 7–9   phase 4 = weeks 10–12

WRESTLING

MODE: PLYOMETRICS

MODE	EXERCISE	*phase 1	phase 2	phase 3	phase 4
Jumping	Pogo, p. 121	3x8-12	3x8-12		
Jumping	Squat Jump, p. 122	3x3-6	3x3-6		
Jumping	Double-Leg Slide Kick, p. 123		3x3-6	3x3-6	3x3-6
Jumping	Knee Tuck Jump, p. 124		3x3-6	3x3-6	3x3-6
Jumping	Split Jump, p. 125		2x4-8	2x4-8	2x4-8
Jumping	Scissor Jump, p. 126		2x6-12	2x6-12	2x6-12
Jumping	Depth Jump, p. 127				2x6-12
Bounding	Prance, p. 128	3x8-12	3x8-12	3x8-12	
Bounding	Gallop, p. 129	2x8-12	2x8-12	2x8-12	
Bounding	Fast Skip, p. 130	3x8-12	3x8-12	3x8-12	
Bounding	Power Skip, p. 130		3x3-6	3x3-6	
Bounding	Ankle Flip, p. 131		2x8-12	3x8-12	3x8-12
Bounding	Bounding, p. 132				2x8-12
Bounding	Lateral Bounding, p. 133	3x4-6	3x4-6	3x4-6	
Hopping	Double-Leg Hops, p. 134		3x3-6	3x3-6	3x3-6
Hopping	Side Hops, p. 135		3x3-6	3x3-6	3x3-6
Hopping	Single-Leg Pogo, p. 136			3x3-6	3x3-6
Hopping	Single-Leg Slide Kick, p. 137				3x3-6
Hopping	Single-Leg Hops, p. 138				3x3-6
Hopping	Diagonal Hops, p. 139				3x3-6
Hopping	Lateral Hops, p. 140				2x3-6
Tosses/Throws	Shovel Toss, p. 141	2x5	2x5	2x5	
Tosses/Throws	Scoop Toss, p. 142	2x5	2x5	2x5	
Tosses/Throws	Twist Toss, p. 143	2x6	2x6	2x6	
Tosses/Throws	Scoop Throw, p. 144		2x5	2x5	2x5
Tosses/Throws	Diagonal Throw, p. 145			2x6	2x6
Tosses/Throws	Kneeling Forward Throw, p. 146		1x5	1x5	1x5
Tosses/Throws	Standing Forward Throw, p. 147		1x5	1x5	1x5
Tosses/Throws	Stepping Forward Throw, p. 148				
Push-Ups	Wall Push-Up, p. 149	2x5	2x5		
Push-Ups	Drop Push-Up, p. 150	2x5	2x5		
Push-Ups	Kneeling Chest Pass, p. 151			2x5	2x5
Push-Ups	Chest Pass, p. 152			2x5	2x5

		Phase 1 (weeks 1–3)	Phase 2 (weeks 4–6)	Phase 3 (weeks 7–9)	Phase 4 (weeks 10–12)
COMPLEXES					
	Good Morning/Overhead Press/Overhead Squat, pp. 95, 109, 100	3x5-8	3x5-8	3x5-8	3x5-8
	Front Squat/Jerk, pp. 102, 118	5x2-4	5x2-4	3x2-4	3x2-4
	Power Clean/Scoop Toss, pp. 117, 142		3x2-4	3x2-4	3x2-4
	Lunge/Split Jump, pp. 66, 125		2x4-8	2x4-8	
COMBOS					
	Clean & Jerk, p. 118		4x1-3	4x1-3	4x1-3
	Front Squat & Jerk, pp. 102, 118			4x1-3	4x1-3
	Overhead Press/Overhead Squat, pp. 109, 100		3x5-8	3x5-8	3x5-8
	Clean & Front Squat & Jerk, pp. 116, 102, 118		4x1-3	4x1-3	4x1-3
SPRINT TRAINING					
Starts	Squared Step, p. 153	2x/leg	2x/leg	2x/leg	
	Staggered Step, p. 153	2x/side	2x/side	2x/side	2x/side
	Open Step, p. 154	2x/side	2x/side	2x/side	2x/side
	Crossover Step, p. 154		2x/side	2x/side	2x/side
	Drop Step, p. 155	2x/side	2x/side	2x/side	2x/side
	Pivot Step, p. 155				2x/side
	Balanced Starts, p. 156		2x/side	2x/side	2x/side
	Resisted Starts, p. 157		2x/side	2x/side	2x/side
	"A" Walk, p. 158	2x20yds	2x20yds	2x20yds	2x20yds
Acceleration	"A" Skip, p. 158	2x20yds	2x20yds	2x20yds	2x20yds
	Wall Drill, p. 160	2x6-10	2x6-10	2x6-10	2x6-10
	"A" Run (Slide kick), p. 158	2x20yds	2x20yds	2x20yds	2x20yds
Speed	"B" Walk, p. 161				
	"B" Skip, p. 161				
	Cadence Fast Leg, p. 162				
AGILITY					
	Sit Drill, p. 163	1x6	1x6	1x6	
	Sway Drill, p. 164			1x6	1x6
	Speed Weave, p. 166		4-6x	4-6x	4-6x
	Shuttle Run, p. 167	4-6x	4-6x	4-6x	4-6x
	Power Weave, p. 168		4-6x	4-6x	4-6x
	3-Cone "L" Run, p. 169		4-6x	4-6x	4-6x
	Directional Drill, p. 170		4-6x	4-6x	4-6x

*phase 1 = weeks 1–3   phase 2 = weeks 4–6   phase 3 = weeks 7–9   phase 4 = weeks 10–12

part three:

the

exercises

top o' the head drill—knee grab

OBJECTIVE *Improves postural extension and hip flexion at a walking pace*

STARTING POSITION: Stand tall with good posture, making sure you do not "sit" or sag throughout the drill.

starting position

1 Step forward with your left foot while lifting and grabbing your right knee, pulling it high and tight to your chest. At the same time, rise onto the toe of your left foot, reaching the top of your head as high as you can without the foot actually leaving the ground.

2 Release your knee and make sure you land on your entire foot, with your weight forward on the foot. Your shin should be over your instep rather than over your heel.

Take a step and repeat on the other side. Continue alternating legs.

top o' the head drill—froggie

OBJECTIVE *Improves postural extension and lateral hip flexion*

STARTING POSITION: Stand tall with good posture, clasping your hands in front of you.

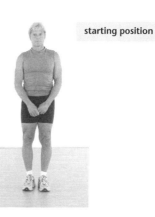

starting position

1 Step forward with your right foot and drive your left knee up and out to the side, above waist level. At the same time, rise onto the toe of your right foot, reaching the top of your head as high as you can without the foot actually leaving the ground.

2 Swing your left knee in front of your chest then step down, as if walking across a large log.

Repeat on the other side.

top o' the head drill—march

OBJECTIVE *Improves postural extension and elevated hip flexion*

STARTING POSITION: Stand tall with good posture, your arms extended in front of you at eye level. Make sure you do not "sit" or sag throughout the drill.

1 Step forward with your right foot, rising onto your right toe as you raise your left leg so that the foot touches your left hand. Reach the top of your head as high as you can.

2 As you step down with your left foot, keep your toes pointing up. At the same time, pull your leg back underneath to contact the ground, keeping your weight forward on that foot.

OBJECTIVE *Improves hip mobility and dorsiflexion of the foot, dynamically stretches the calf, prevents shin splint*

STARTING POSITION: Assume a normal walking posture.

starting position

1 Lock your knees and step forward with your right foot, dorsiflexing your ankle (pointing your toes toward your knees) so that only the heel contacts the ground.

2 Repeat on the other side and continue walking this way for 30 yards.

Gradually increase the distance weekly to 150 yards.

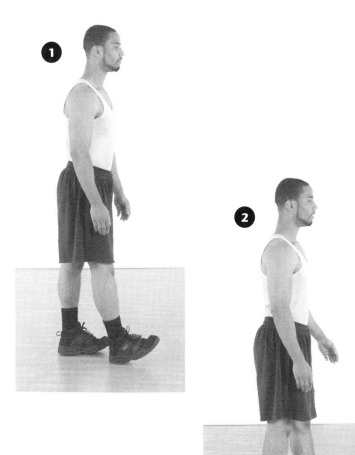

toe walk

OBJECTIVE *Improves hip mobility, dynamically stretches the shin, strengthens the ankle and calf muscles*

STARTING POSITION: Assume a normal walking posture.

starting position

1 Lock your knees and step forward with your left foot, plantar-flexing the ankle (pointing your toes down) so that only the toes and the ball of the foot contact the ground.

Repeat on the other side and continue walking this way.

toe grab

OBJECTIVE *Improves hip flexion, dynamically stretches the back side of the leg and low back*

STARTING POSITION: Assume a normal walking posture.

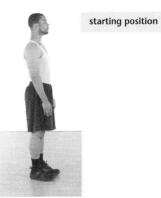

starting position

1 Keeping your legs straight, step forward with your right foot dorsiflexed (toes up).

2 Hinge your torso at the hips and grab your right toe with your left hand.

Walk a couple of steps and repeat on the other side, alternating leg and hand.

dynamic warm-up
forward lunge

OBJECTIVE *Improves hip mobility, dynamically stretches the glutes, hamstrings and hip extensors, improves posture, strengthens the core*

STARTING POSITION: Assume a normal walking posture.

starting position

1 Step forward with your right foot and bend your back leg until the knee gently touches the ground directly under the hip. Keep your shoulders over your hips and back knee.

2 Push off with your back leg to stride through and repeat the lunge on the other side.

Alternate for prescribed repetitions.

BACKWARD LUNGE

Instead of stepping forward with your right leg, step backward and bend your right knee until it gently touches the ground directly under the hip. This challenges your balance a bit more.

side-to-side lunge

OBJECTIVE *Improves hip mobility, dynamically stretches the glutes, hamstrings and groin muscles, improves posture, strengthens the core*

STARTING POSITION: Assume a normal walking posture.

starting position

1 Pushing off with your slightly flexed left leg, step forward with your right foot. Pivot on the left foot to face sideways when the right foot lands. Keep your chest open and your shoulders over your hips.

2 Repeat on the other side, pushing off and stepping forward with the left foot. Pivot on the right foot to face the opposite side.

dynamic warm-up
hands & heels

OBJECTIVE *Improves hip mobility, dynamically stretches the muscles of the legs, low back and shoulder, strengthens the core*

STARTING POSITION: Assume a normal walking posture.

starting position

1 Hinging at your hips and keeping the heels of both feet on the ground, reach forward until the palms of both hands are on the ground.

2 Keep your hips high, your legs straight and your hands on the floor as you step forward with your left leg.

Continue crawling forward.

MOUNTAIN CLIMB VARIATION

To further strengthen your hip flexors and extensors, in Step 2, step forward with your right foot, bending your hip and knee so that your foot lands fully past your right hand.

exaggerated skip

OBJECTIVE *Improves hip mobility, dynamically stretches the muscles of the legs, low back and shoulders, increases the tempo of the movement progression*

This drill uses a step-hop-step-hop rhythmic manner. The steps should be of good stride and the hops very quick.

STARTING POSITION: Assume a normal walking posture.

starting position

1 Begin skipping by stepping with your right foot and swinging your left knee above hip height. Clap your hands beneath your thigh.

Continue skipping and clapping, alternating sides.

VARIATION 1: Include exaggerated arm swings both backward and upward for increased mobilization of the torso.

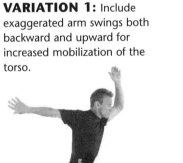

CROSSOVER SKIP VARIATION: As the skipping knee comes up, drive it upward and inward to the midline of the body.

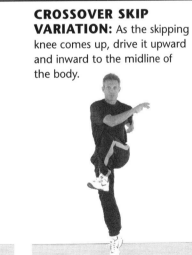

OBJECTIVE *Improves hip, knee and ankle mobility, dynamically stretches the groin and hamstrings*

STARTING POSITION: Stand with your feet approximately hip-width apart, knees slightly bent. Your feet should point straight ahead and your hips should stay level throughout the drill.

starting position

1 Push your left foot into the ground, driving your right knee and hip to the right.

2 Immediately land with your right foot and gather your left foot back under the hip to repeat. Your hips should remain low as your feet glide along the ground.

VARIATION: Swing and rhythmically circle the arms simultaneously.

lateral skip

OBJECTIVE *Improves hip, knee and ankle mobility, dynamically stretches the groin and hamstrings, improve lateral push mechanics and hip projection*

STARTING POSITION: Stand with your feet approximately hip-width apart, knees slightly bent. Your feet should point straight ahead and your hips should stay level throughout the drill.

starting position

1 Push off with your left foot to skip, sending your hips to the right. Land again on your left foot and push your hips to the right again.

2 Land the skip on your right foot.

Do this hop-on-the-left/step-with-the-right movement (left-left-right, left-left-right) for the prescribed distance. Then repeat in the opposite direction for a right-foot hop, left-foot step (right-right-left, right-right-left) sequence. The steps should be of good stride and the hops very quick.

dynamic warm-up
carioca

OBJECTIVE *Increases mobility of the rotational aspects of the hips, knees and ankles, dynamically stretches the groin, hamstrings and trunk muscles*

STARTING POSITION: Stand with your feet hip-width apart, knees slightly bent. Keep your center of gravity low and your hips loose throughout the drill.

starting position

1

2

1 Step your right foot in front of and across your left leg. Continuing in the same direction, step your left leg to the left so that you're once again in a wide stance.

2 Step your right foot in back of and across your left leg.

Continue this step-behind/step/step-in-front movement for the prescribed distance, then switch directions.

VARIATION: Stand taller and have the knee cross over above the waist.

backward run

OBJECTIVE *Improves mobility of the hips and low back, dynamically stretches the hip flexors and quadriceps, develops opposing muscles and balances out the run load*

If this movement was caught on film, it would look as if someone were just reversing forward running. This drill is used a great deal in cooldown as well.

STARTING POSITION: Assume a normal running posture.

starting position

1 Holding your torso exactly as you would when running forward, run backward by leading with your feet, reaching your heels back and trying to gain as much ground with each stride as possible.

OBJECTIVE *Improves mobility of the hips and low back, dynamically stretches the quadriceps and hamstrings, develops ability to move in a low-hip set position with feet staying beneath the center of gravity*

STARTING POSITION: Stand with your hips and knees bent, keeping your shoulders positioned over your knees. Maintain this position throughout the drill. Your back should be arched, not rounded.

starting position

1 Move backward by leading with your hips and picking your knees upward, not reaching your heels back; make sure your feet remain under your hips. Pump your elbows backward and forward as if you were running forward.

backward skip

OBJECTIVE *Improves mobility of the hips and low back, dynamically stretches the quadriceps, glutes and hamstrings, enhances the ability to move quickly with backward "push" mechanics and the feet staying beneath the center of gravity*

STARTING POSITION: Stand with your hips and knees bent, keeping your shoulders positioned over your knees. Your back should be arched.

starting position

1 Keeping your torso held high, step back with your right foot and hop on that foot, pumping your arms naturally.

2 Step back with your left foot and hop on that foot.

Continue the right-right, left-left cadence.

backward shuffle

OBJECTIVE *Improves mobility of the hips, knees and ankles, dynamically stretches the glutes, groin and hamstrings*

This drill includes rotational movements at the hip to maintain a forward sightline with linear backward movement.

STARTING POSITION: Using a 10–15-yard distance, imagine a board or log placed across it. Take a hip-width stance on the imaginary board with your eyes focused on the starting point.

starting position

1 Perform two shuffle steps to the right, away from the starting point and down the imaginary board.

2–3 Upon completion of the second shuffle, step and pivot around without turning your back to the starting point.

Now perform two shuffle steps to the left, continuing down the imaginary board backwards away from the starting point, but never losing sight of it.

OBJECTIVE *Creates a solid, stable foundation throughout the torso, employs quality extension at the hip joint*

STARTING POSITION: Looking forward, place only your forearms and toes on the ground. Your body should form a straight line from shoulders to ankles.

starting position

1 Lifting from your hip, not your knee, raise your left leg as high as possible. Keep the leg long and maintain the pedestal posture.

Do prescribed repetitions, then switch legs.

core training
supine pedestal

OBJECTIVE *Creates a solid, stable foundation throughout the torso, employs quality flexion at the hip joint*

STARTING POSITION: Facing the ceiling, place only your forearms and heels on the ground. Your body should form a straight line from shoulders to ankles.

starting position

1 Lifting from your hip, not your knee, raise your left leg as high as possible. Keep the leg long and maintain the pedestal posture.

Do prescribed repetitions, then switch legs.

OBJECTIVE *Creates a solid, stable foundation throughout the torso, employs quality abduction at the hip joint.*

STARTING POSITION: Place your left forearm and the outer edge of your left foot on the ground, then stack your feet, hips and shoulders so that your body completely faces the side. Your left elbow should be beneath your left shoulder, and your torso should be in a straight line from shoulders to ankles, and from nose to toes.

starting position

1 Raise your right leg as high as possible, keeping it long and maintaining a straight torso.

Do prescribed repetitions, then switch sides.

> **VARIATION:** If you need additional support, you can place your other hand on the ground.

starting position

OBJECTIVE *Creates a solid, stable foundation throughout the torso, strengthens the neck and shoulders*

STARTING POSITION: Stand with your body as rigid and straight as possible, keeping your feet together and arms at your sides. Your partner stands on your left side and cups his hands around your left ear.

1 Have your partner take a step backward, away from you, as you tilt from your ankles to your left. He will be supporting your weight in his hands. Maintain your rigid torso without losing balance or rotating.

2 Your partner will take more steps backward, lowering you toward the ground as long as you can maintain your rigid torso and balance.

Once you have reached a challenging point, your partner will step back towards you, raising you back to the starting position. Switch sides.

VARIATION:
This procedure can also be performed to the front and the back, with the partner supporting at the forehead and back of the head, respectively.

back-to-back squat

OBJECTIVE *Creates a stable yet mobile foundation throughout the torso, employs quality flexion and extension at the hip, knee and ankle joints*

Although this drill can be done with your back against the wall, you enhance your posture and balance more by working with a partner.

STARTING POSITION: Stand back-to-back with your partner and interlock your elbows. Make sure your feet are in full contact with the ground throughout the exercise.

starting position

1 Keeping back contact, bend your knees and lower your hips until they are below knee level.

2 Push back against your partner to extend back up to the starting position.

OBJECTIVE *Creates a stable yet mobile foundation throughout the torso, employs quality flexion and extension at the hip, knee and ankle joints*

Although this can be done by holding on to a rail or a bar, you enhance your posture and balance more by working with a partner.

STARTING POSITION: Face your partner and grab his right hand/wrist with your right, his left hand/wrist with your left. Place the toes of both feet against the toes of your partner. Keep full foot contact with the ground and your arms extended throughout the movement.

starting position

1

1 Bend your knees and lower your hips until your hips are below knee level.

2 Maintaining leverage against your partner, extend back up to the starting position.

2

twisting lunge

OBJECTIVE *Creates a stable foundation throughout the torso, success-fully flexes, extends and rotates the body in coordination with forward movement*

STARTING POSITION: Standing with your feet hip-width apart, hold a medicine ball, keeping your elbows at your sides.

starting position

1 As you step forward with your right foot into a full lunge, touching your back knee lightly to the ground directly beneath your hips and shoulders, twist to your right. Make sure your shoulders turn with the ball.

2 Extend up and, without pausing at the top, step your back leg through to the front for the lunge and twist.

Alternate sides for prescribed repetitions.

VARIATION: To increase the challenge, extend your arms, holding the ball farther away from your body throughout the twist.

BACKWARD LUNGE VARIATION: Rather than step forward, step backward with your right foot into a full lunge, touching your right knee lightly to the ground directly beneath the hips and shoulders, twist to your left. This challenges the flexion, extension and rotation of the body in coordination with backward movement.

core training
overhead reach

OBJECTIVE *Creates a stable foundation throughout the torso, successfully flexes, extends and rotates the body in coordination with exaggerated stepping movement*

STARTING POSITION: Standing with your feet hip-width apart, hold a medicine ball high above your head.

starting position

1 As you step forward with your right foot into a full lunge, touching the back knee lightly to the ground directly beneath your hips and shoulders, lower the ball to your right. Keep your arms lengthened.

Extend up, bringing the ball up overhead, and, without pausing, step your back leg through to the front for the lunge and lower the ball to the left.

Alternate sides for prescribed repetitions.

VARIATION: Instead of simply raising and lowering the ball, you can also circle it around in coordination with your step: As your left foot steps forward, circle the ball from the right, towards the front, and then to the left; as your right foot steps forward, you would continue circling the ball behind you and then to the right.

duck walk

OBJECTIVE *Creates a strong, mobile foundation through the hips and lower torso*

STARTING POSITION: Stand with your feet hip-width apart. Bend your knees and lower your hips as if you were going to sit In a low chair. Keep your torso long and wide and your shoulders back.

starting position

1 Keeping this squat position the entire time, take a small step forward with your right foot, making sure that your whole foot takes off and lands fully and stays beneath your torso.

2 Take a step with your left foot, again lifting the whole foot.

BACKWARD DUCK WALK VARIATION:
Instead of moving forward, take small steps backward. The steps are even shorter for this style.

russian (cossack) duck walk

OBJECTIVE *Creates a strong, mobile foundation through the hips and lower torso, and improves hamstring strength and flexibility*

STARTING POSITION: Stand with your feet hip-width apart. Bend your knees and lower your hips as if you were going to sit In a low chair. Keep your torso long and wide and your shoulders back. Extend your arms in front of you at eye level.

starting position

1

1 Maintaining this squat position throughout the drill, take a short step forward with your right foot and lift the toes so that they come in contact with your right hand. Your foot should land beneath your torso.

2 Take a step with your left foot, lifting the toes so that they come in contact with your left hand.

2

single-arm push-up

OBJECTIVE *Employs total body core stabilization utilizing the upper torso, improves shoulder strength, mobility and dynamic pressing*

STARTING POSITION: Assume a push-up position with one hand on a medicine ball. Your body should form a straight line from shoulders to ankles.

starting position

1 Lower your chest to the floor.

2 Maintaining the pedestal position, push back up to the starting position, making sure to extend both arms fully.

VARIATION: To increase the one-arm challenge, once you've pushed up, roll the ball over to the other arm and perform the next push-up. As you improve, you should be able to speed up to the point that the ball remains in the middle and the arms rapidly push back and forth.

double-arm push-up

OBJECTIVE *Employs total body core stabilization utilizing the upper torso, improves shoulder strength, mobility and dynamic pressing*

STARTING POSITION: Assume a push-up position with both hands on a medicine ball. Your body should form a straight line from shoulders to ankles.

starting position

1

1 Lower your chest to the ball.

2 Maintaining the pedestal position, push back up to the starting position, making sure to extend both arms fully.

2

VARIATION: To increase the challenge, bring your feet closer together or cross one ankle over the other.

over & under

OBJECTIVE *Improves balance and stability through full flexion and extension of the torso*

STARTING POSITION: Stand with your feet hip-width apart, knees bent. Hold the medicine ball in front of you with both hands. Your partner stands behind you.

starting position

1 Lift the ball directly overhead and pass it to your partner.

2–3 Keeping your feet in full contact with the ground, squat down and bend at the waist to grab the ball from between your legs.

medicine ball twist

OBJECTIVE *Improves balance and stability through rotation of the torso*

STARTING POSITION: Stand back to back with your partner, your feet hip-width apart and your knees bent. Hold the medicine ball in front of you with both hands.

starting position

1 Keeping your knees bent and your feet in full contact with the ground, twist to the right to pass the ball to your partner, who is twisting to the same side (his left).

2 Twist to the other side to receive the ball.

VARIATION: To increase the challenge and get a fuller twist, twist to your left as your partner twists to his left.

OBJECTIVE *Improves balance and stability employing the skills of catching and tossing*

This drill can also be done against a wall.

STARTING POSITION: Hold a ball in both hands and stand facing your partner, who is facing you. You and your partner raise your left knee to hip height, keeping your heel just in front of your right knee, toe up towards knee.

starting position

1

2

1 Toss the ball to your partner.

2 Catch the ball as your partner throws it back, maintaining your one-legged position.

Your partner should throw the ball back from different angles.

Repeat prescribed number of tosses, then switch legs.

VARIATION: Try this by having one side face the wall, then the other. Progress to tossing and catching from positions to the side and behind.

core training
back walkover

OBJECTIVE *Enhances strength and mobility through the torso*

This can also be done against a railing or wall.

STARTING POSITION: Stand with your back against a sturdy object.

starting position

1 Take two large steps away from it and, keeping the toes of both feet on the same line and the knees out over the toes, bend over backwards.

2 Keeping your feet in full contact with the ground, press your hands against the object, fingers pointing toward the ground.

3 Walk your hands down the object until your head touches the ground. Maintain a well-arched back and walk back up the wall to a standing position.

OBJECTIVE *Enhances strength and mobility throughout the entire torso*

This can also be done with a bar or railing.

STARTING POSITION: Grab the back of a sturdy chair that is approximately shoulder level. Walk your feet back until your arms are hanging, fully extended, and your toes are the only body part touching the ground.

starting position

1–2 From this full hang, pull yourself up and then push yourself away.

During the first few attempts, you may feel as if you may break in half. Soon you should be able to push away with enough power to regain your standing position.

core training
single-leg squat

OBJECTIVE *Enhance strength and stability through the torso, improves the same posture, balance and mobility in the ankle, knee and hip that are used throughout movements of agility*

STARTING POSITION: Stand with your right knee bent, raising the foot behind you above knee level.

starting position

1 Keeping an upright posture and your right foot in full contact with the ground, lower your hips until your right knee touches the ground. Be sure the heel of the support foot never leaves the ground.

2 Slowly return to the starting position.

Perform prescribed reps then switch legs.

VARIATION: Begin this drill while holding on to the back of a chair. This is the proper progression for technical success.

VARIATION: Once you're proficient at the free-standing version, try this movement flexed at the hip rather than at the knee.

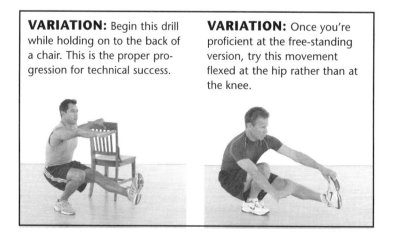

OBJECTIVE *Enhances hip movement, strengthens the muscles of the low back and hamstrings for starting, jumping and sprinting*

STARTING POSITION: Stand with a light to moderate barbell on the back of your shoulders, knees slightly flexed and feet narrower than hip-width apart.

starting position

1

1 Imagine a table placed against the middle of your thighs. Hinging at the hip and keeping the arch in your back, lay your chest on this imaginary table. Make sure your center of gravity stays over the instep or mid-portion of your feet so they stay in full contact with the floor. Proper form will allow you to feel like you could jump from any position in this movement.

2 Return to starting position using the muscles of your low back and hamstrings.

2

OBJECTIVE *Enhances hip movement, strengthens the muscles of the low back and hamstrings for starting, jumping and sprinting*

STARTING POSITION: Stand with your knees slightly flexed and feet narrower than hip-width apart. Hold a light to moderate barbell at arm's length in front of your thighs.

starting position

1 Imagine a table placed against the middle of your thighs. Hinging at the hips and keeping the arch in your back, lay your chest on this imaginary table. Make sure the barbell stays close to your legs and directly over your shoe laces, and that your feet are in full contact with the floor. Proper form will allow you to feel like you could jump from any position in this movement.

2 Return to starting position using the muscles of your low back and hamstrings.

OBJECTIVE *Enhances power through the torso, strengthens the low back and hamstrings, improves flexion into extension for starting, jumping, sprinting and weightlifting*

Not to be confused with a Romanian deadlift.

STARTING POSITION: Stand with your knees slightly flexed and feet hip-width apart. Place a barbell on the floor next to your shins. Hinging at the hips and keeping the arch in your back, grab the barbell. Keep the barbell over your shoe laces and your feet fully on the floor.

starting position

1 Keeping your arms relaxed, your wrists forward and your elbows slightly outward so that the bar stays close to your legs, slowly straighten back up until the bar reaches high thigh level.

2 Quickly "shrug" your body long and tall. Think "shoulders in the ear, hips tall and high up on the toes" as the bar rises up through an imaginary belt buckle.

3 Slowly return the bar to the floor with the same posture.

clean pull

OBJECTIVE *Improves power through the torso, strengthens the shoulders, hips and legs, increases flexion into maximum extension for starting, jumping, sprinting and weightlifting*

STARTING POSITION: Stand with your feet hip-width apart, grasping a barbell directly above your shoe laces. Keeping your chest wide, your back arched, and your feet fully on the ground, squat down until your knees are bent well over the bar and your body weight is over your insteps.

starting position

1 With your hips and shoulders rising at the same time, pull the bar to high thigh level and shift your knees forward into a jump position.

2–3 Quickly "shrug" your body long and tall, jumping without your toes leaving the ground. Shrug your shoulders to your ears with your elbows outward. Think "hips tall and high up on the toes" as the bar rises up through an imaginary belt buckle.

OBJECTIVE *Improves power through the torso, strengthens the shoulders, hips and legs, increases flexion into maximum extension for starting, jumping, sprinting and weightlifting*

STARTING POSITION: Stand tall with your feet hip-width apart, holding a barbell directly above your shoe laces; keep your hands wide apart on the bar to emphasize the shrugging movement. Keeping your chest wide, your back arched, and your feet fully on the ground, squat down until your knees are bent well over the bar and your body weight is over your insteps.

starting position

1 With your hips and shoulders rising at the same time, pull the bar to high thigh level and shift your knees forward into a jump position.

2 Quickly "shrug" your body long and tall, jumping without your toes leaving the ground. Think "shoulders in the ear, hips tall and high up on the toes" as the bar rises up through an imaginary belt buckle.

3 Once the bar is shrugged past the hips, continue to pull your elbows high above your shoulders. Think "hips high, elbows high." Make sure your elbows are over the bar rather than behind.

OBJECTIVE *Improves core strength throughout the legs and torso, sets the posture, balance and mobility for all squatting movements*

STARTING POSITION: Stand with your feet hip-width apart, toes outward. Hold a barbell at arm's length overhead. Your grip may need to be wide to allow shoulder rotation.

starting position

1 Keeping your elbows locked and in line with your feet, inhale to bend your knees and lower your hips back until they are below knee level. Keep your feet flat on the ground the entire time and make sure to maintain an arched back to assure better squat posture and mobility.

2 Exhale to return to starting position.

OBJECTIVE *Improves core strength throughout the legs and torso, develops the areas that are used in hiking, climbing, running and sprinting*

STARTING POSITION: Stand tall with your feet hip-width apart and hold a barbell at arm's length overhead. Your grip may need to be wide to allow shoulder rotation.

starting position

1 Inhaling, lunge forward with your right leg so that your entire foot is flat on the ground and your knee is bent over the instep of the foot; lower your back knee gently to the ground. Keep the barbell in line with your ears, shoulders, hips and back knee.

2 Exhale to push back up to the starting position without the front heel dragging.

Alternate steps for prescribed number of repetitions.

VARIATION: Rather than pushing your front leg back to the starting position, you can step forward with your back foot into the starting position.

OBJECTIVE *Improves core strength throughout the legs and torso, challenges posture, balance and mobility with the use of greater load*

STARTING POSITION: Stand tall with your feet hip-width apart. Holding the barbell with a relaxed grip, rest the barbell on the front of your shoulders and let the bar sit back on your fingers. Keep your elbows forward and lifted high.

starting position

1 Inhaling, bend your knees and lower your hips back until they are below knee level.

2 Exhale to return to the starting position.

FRONT LUNGE VARIA-TION: With the barbell on the front of your shoulders, you can also move into a lunge.

BACK SQUAT AND LUNGE VARIATION: The barbell is placed on the back of the shoulders. Once in this position, move into a squat or a lunge (pictured).

OBJECTIVE *Improves core strength throughout the legs and torso*

The single-leg nature of this drill can allow for quality strength work using less load on the shoulders and low back. This is part of a quality training progression for rehabilitation and/or beginning squat and acceleration training.

STARTING POSITION: Select a platform that is below knee level and place your right foot on top. Hold dumbbells either in your hands or a barbell on the back of your shoulders.

starting position

1–2 Imagine a raw egg taped to the bottom of your left foot. Without "breaking the egg," arch your back and straighten your right leg so that you're standing on the platform.

Slowly lower your hips and left heel back to the ground. Repeat prescribed number of repetitions then switch legs.

step-up with push-off

The lower leg does the majority of the work. This version involves a considerably heavier load.

STARTING POSITION: Place your right foot on top of the plyo box. Hold a barbell on the back of your shoulders.

starting position

1–2 Flex your left leg and powerfully straighten it to drive the hip up to a balanced position on the right leg. Lower the left leg.

Repeat prescribed number of repetitions then switch legs.

Both legs work together to extend the hip high up onto the platform. The load is moderate.

STARTING POSITION: Hold a barbell on the back of your shoulders and poise your right foot to step on the plyo box.

1

starting position

1 As you step your right foot onto the platform, raise your left knee to above hip level. This toe-up, knee-up action should lift the hip and extend the right leg onto the toes. Think "hips high start to a hips higher finish."

Lower the left leg back to the floor. Alternate sides for pre-scribed number of repetitions.

STEP-UP EXPLOSIVE VARIATION: This is performed exactly like the knee-drive with such speed and drive that the foot leaves the platform in a jump. Alternate the legs of this high-quality jumping step-up for 4–6 total reps.

The goal here is explosive extension of the hips without knee drive. The load is light.

STARTING POSITION: Hold a barbell on the back of your shoulders and place your right foot on top of the plyo box.

starting position

1 Push off with both feet, straightening your legs so that you explode high above the platform.

2 Switch your legs in the air and land your left foot lightly on the platform.

3 As soon as your right foot touches the ground, explode off the platform using both legs.

Alternate sides for prescribed number of repetitions.

OBJECTIVE *Improves core strength, balance and stability in the torso and legs for beginning single-leg squatting and ankle, knee and/or hip rehabilitation*

You will need a paper cup for this drill.

STARTING POSITION: Place a paper cup on its side to the left of a mid-calf-level platform. With your right leg, stand on the edge of the platform, keeping your left leg and foot suspended out to the side.

starting position

1 Keeping your chest wide and your back arched, bend your right knee over your toes and lower your left foot to the paper cup. Your goal is to touch the cup without bending or squashing it.

2 Straighten back up to the starting position.

Do prescribed number of repetitions then switch legs.

single-leg squat (loaded)

OBJECTIVE *Strengthens the legs without heavily loading the shoulders and low back*

This is an excellent drill for sprinting, jumping and cutting movements.

STARTING POSITION: Stand with the back of both legs against a bench or platform that is calf height. Hold a barbell either in both hands or on your shoulders.

starting position

1 Take a moderate stride forward with your right foot and place the instep of your left foot on the platform. This is to restrict the use of your back leg.

2 Bend your right knee and lower your hips until your left knee touches the ground. The load should remain in line with your back knee to assure proper posture.

Do prescribed number of repetitions then switch legs.

VARIATION: To increase the challenge to your posture and stability, hold the barbell in front of the shoulders, and then locked out overhead during the entire squatting sequence.

overhead press

OBJECTIVE *Strengthens the upper torso, improves stability and mobility in the shoulders*

This combination of a behind-the-neck press and a military press is an excellent lead-in for all of the standing push progressions.

STARTING POSITION: Stand with your feet hip-width apart and your knees slightly bent, holding a barbell on the back of your shoulders. Keep your chest wide and hips cocked back throughout the exercise.

starting position

1 Keeping your elbows underneath the barbell, extend your arms upward until your elbows lock out.

2 Lower the barbell onto the front of your shoulders and repeat the press. Continue alternating lowering the barbell onto your shoulder in front and behind the head. Regardless of the starting position your arms should always lock out behind your ears in the finished position.

push press

OBJECTIVE *Strengthens the torso, improves powerful pushing techniques as used in combative sports like wrestling, football, basketball, rugby, hockey and martial arts*

STARTING POSITION: Stand with your feet hip-width apart and your knees slightly bent, holding a barbell on your shoulders. Keep your elbows forward and lifted high.

starting position

1 Bending your knees slightly to drop your hips straight down, push with your legs to drive the barbell up off your shoulders.

2 As your legs become almost fully extended, vigorously press the bar up until your arms lock out. In this "drive" phase, the heels may leave the ground momentarily but not the toes.

3 Press out to finish.

OBJECTIVE *Strengthens the torso, increases reactive speed in pushing techniques as used in combative sports that utilize jumping, shoving and throwing*

STARTING POSITION: Stand with your feet hip-width apart and your knees slightly bent, holding a barbell on your shoulders. Keep your chest wide and hips cocked back throughout the exercise.

starting position

1 Bend your knees slightly to drop your hips straight down, then rapidly push with your legs to drive the barbell up off your shoulders.

2 As your legs and hips become almost fully extended, driving your feet off the ground, vigorously push yourself under the bar and immediately lock your arms out. Your body is "punched" into a flexed position underneath the bar.

3 Land with both knees bent and your feet flat on the ground, your arms locked out past your ears. Squat the bar upward to a full standing position and stabilize the weight overhead.

OBJECTIVE *Strengthens the torso, enhances foot and leg speed for pushing movements used in combative sports that utilize jumping, shoving and throwing.*

STARTING POSITION: Stand with your feet hip-width apart and your knees slightly bent, holding a barbell on either the front or back of your shoulders. Keep your chest wide and hips cocked back throughout the exercise.

starting position

1 Bending your knees slightly to drop your hips straight down, push with your legs to drive the barbell up off your shoulders.

2 Drive your feet off the ground by rapidly extending your legs and hips...

3 ...and vigorously push yourself under the bar up until your arms lock out, driving your body underneath the bar by splitting one leg forward and the other leg back.

4 Return to the starting position by stepping your left foot next to your right.

Alternate split legs.

OBJECTIVE *Improves starting strength and overall power, improves coordination in starting, jumping, throwing, kicking, rowing, swimming, diving and sprinting*

Caution: For best results, this Olympic-style lift must be done with an Olympic bar. Other bars can be used, but bars without sleeves that spin create technique and performance problems. Regardless of age, fitness level and weight-training experience, always pay strict attention to alignment and posture.

STARTING POSITION: With your feet hip-width apart and the barbell directly above your shoe laces, squat down and grab the bar so that your wrists, knees and shoulders are in front of the bar. Keep your hands wide apart on the bar to emphasize the shrugging movement. Your body weight should be balanced over your insteps.

starting position

1 Slowly start pulling on the bar, your hips and shoulders simultaneously rising as the bar slides up the shins past your knees.

2 The pull speeds up as you shift your knees forward, shrug your shoulders and "scoop" the bar off of your hips. Jump and finish the pull with a shrug by bringing your elbows high and over the bar.

3–4 Pull your body under the bar, landing full-footed with your toes pointing slightly outward, and lock out your elbows.

To return to starting position, lower the bar to your chest, then rotate your elbows back to release the bar to the floor.

VARIATIONS: You can also try this by placing the barbell on blocks that position the bar just above or below your knees. These assist in the starting power of the different pull positions.

The *power snatch* is pulling well enough to not have to squat fully underneath in order to catch the bar; the load will generally be lighter than that used with the full snatch. Eventually, progressive load should dictate that the technique of "finishing the pull" requires catching the bar strong but in lower and lower squat positions. Another variation helpful for sprinters is the *split (landing) snatch*.

OBJECTIVE *Improves starting strength and overall power, improves coordination in starting, jumping, throwing, kicking, rowing, swimming, diving and sprinting*

Caution: For best results, this Olympic-style lift must be done with an Olympic bar. Other bars can be used, but bars without sleeves that spin create technique and performance problems. Regardless of age, fitness level and weight-training experience, always pay strict attention to alignment and posture.

STARTING POSITION: With your feet hip-width apart and the barbell directly above your shoe laces, squat down and grab the bar so that your wrists, knees and shoulders are in front of the bar. Your body weight should be balanced over your insteps.

starting position

1 Slowly start pulling on the bar, your hips and shoulders rising simultaneously as the bar slides up your shins past your knees.

2 The pull speeds up as you shift your knees forward, shrug your shoulders and "scoop" the bar high off of your thigh.

3 Jump and finish the pull with a shrug by bringing your elbows high and over the bar.

4 Relax your grip and pull your body under the bar, landing full-footed with your toes pointed slightly outward. Whip your elbows around and up, and land the bar on your shoulders.

Bring your elbows backward and lower the bar gently below your waist before lowering it to the ground.

VARIATIONS: You can also try this by placing the barbell on blocks that position the bar just above or below your knees. These assist in the starting power of the different pull positions.

The *power clean* is pulling well enough to not have to squat fully underneath in order to catch the bar; the load will generally be lighter than that used with the full squat. Eventually progressive load should dictate that the technique of "finishing the pull" requires catching the bar strong but in lower and lower squat positions.

OBJECTIVE *Improves strength and overall power, improves coordination in starting, jumping, throwing, rowing, swimming, diving and sprinting*

Caution: For best results, this Olympic-style lift must be done with an Olympic bar. Other bars can be used, but bars without sleeves that spin create technique and performance problems. Regardless of age, fitness level and weight-training experience, always pay strict attention to alignment and posture.

STARTING POSITION: With your feet hip-width apart and the barbell directly above your shoe laces, squat down and grab the bar so that your wrists, knees and shoulders are in front of the bar. Your body weight should be balanced over your insteps.

starting position

1 Clean (see page 116) the barbell onto the front of your shoulders.

2 Pause and take a good breath. Reset the grip. Dip straight down by bending your knees and keeping your shoulders directly above your hips.

3–4 Drive straight up and punch your body underneath the bar with either a split or squared (push jerk) stance to lock the bar out above your ears.

Step back into a full standing position, then lower the bar to your shoulders then to the floor.

VARIATIONS: You can combine the moves by doing 1 clean and 1 jerk for 2 reps, or complex the moves by doing 2 cleans followed by 2 jerks.

OBJECTIVE *Improves starting strength and overall power, improves force production for starting, jumping and sprinting*

This can also be done using a barbell.

STARTING POSITION: Stand with your feet hip-width apart, holding a 30- to 50-pound sand bag comfortably on your shoulders.

starting position

1 With good posture and control, bend your knees and lower your hips to knee level.

2 At the bottom of the squat, straighten your legs and drive your hips upward as fast and as powerfully as possible. This should cause your feet to lift well off of the ground.

3 Land full-footed as if you were going to take off immediately, then return to the starting position.

This is a single-response drill, therefore reset between each repetition.

VARIATION: A progression employs a heavier load on the torso (shoulders or hips). Once you're above approximately 30 percent of your body weight with the load, eliminate landing with it. Upon take-off and reaching the maximum height of jump, release the weight and land separate from it.

starting position

OBJECTIVE *Improves foot and ankle mechanics and proper landing in any sprint and jump activity*

This is the beginning exercise in the teaching and learning of jumping.

STARTING POSITION: Stand with your feet hip-width apart, knees slightly bent and elbows back.

1 Take off with both feet and thrust your thumbs upward until they're at eye level (known as blocking with the arms); straighten your legs to project your hips as high in the air as possible.

As you land, make sure to lock your ankles so that your toes point up. Slightly flex your knees and cock your hips and arms, ensuring that the front half of the foot contacts for quick, elastic take-offs.

OBJECTIVE *Improves take-off and landing posture, develops power in the legs and hips*

Progress from single jumps to multiple jumps with pause, then finally multiple jumps without pause.

STARTING POSITION: Stand comfortably with your feet hip-width apart and place your hands behind your head (this will assure proper posture for both take-offs and landings).

starting position

1–2 Bend to a quarter-squat then immediately explode upward as high as possible, straightening your hips, knees and ankles to maximum length.

3 Land on both feet with your locked ankles and knees bent, prepared to take off again.

VARIATION:
As you improve, try this exercise by blocking with your arms (thrusting your thumbs upward until they're at eye level).

OBJECTIVE *Improves transference of force and hip flexion—a key factor in the improvement of sprinting*

Progress from single jumps to multiple jumps with pause, then finally multiple jumps without pause.

STARTING POSITION: Stand comfortably with your feet hip-width apart.

starting position

1 Bend to a quarter-squat then immediately explode upward. Once your hips are as high as possible, drive your knees high toward your chest and then slide your heels upward into the buttocks as if your back were against a wall. Your knees will rise upward as you maintain your posture and upright position by blocking with the arms (thrusting your thumbs upward until they're at eye level).

2 Land on both feet with your locked ankles and knees bent, and your elbows back, prepared to take off again.

power training
knee tuck jump

OBJECTIVE *Improves transference of force and hip flexion—a key factor in the improvement of sprinting and jumping in sports like volleyball, basketball, diving and track & field*

Progress from single jumps to multiple jumps with pause, then finally multiple jumps without pause.

STARTING POSITION: Stand comfortably with your feet hip-width apart and extend your arms, palms down, in front of you at chest height.

starting position

1–2 Dip down to a quarter-squat then immediately explode upward. Once your hips are as high as possible, drive your knees high toward your chest and attempt to touch them to your palms.

Land on both feet with your locked ankles and knees bent, prepared to take off again. Minimize ground contact time.

VARIATION:
As you improve, try this exercise by blocking with your arms (thrusting your thumbs upward until they're at eye level).

OBJECTIVE *Develops striding power for running and cross-country skiing*

This is similar to the "split" portion of the jerk.

STARTING POSITION: Stand with your left leg forward, keeping your front knee over the instep of your left foot and the back knee bent and located beneath your hips and shoulders.

starting position

1 Jump as high and straight up as possible, blocking with your arms to gain additional lift.

2 Land in the split-legged position, bending your knees slightly to absorb the shock.

Repeat then switch legs. This can be performed single response and then progressed to multiple-response mode.

OBJECTIVE *Enhances the muscles of the lower body and torso, emphasizes leg speed*

Attainment of maximal vertical height and leg speed is stressed in this exercise. This drill is especially good for all runner and jumpers.

STARTING POSITION: Stand with your left leg forward, keeping your front knee over the instep of your left foot and the back knee bent and located beneath your hips and shoulders.

starting position

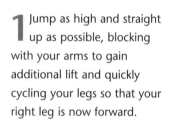

1 Jump as high and straight up as possible, blocking with your arms to gain additional lift and quickly cycling your legs so that your right leg is now forward.

2 Land with your right leg forward in the split-legged position, bending your knees slightly to absorb the shock.

Repeat, cycling the other leg forward. This multiple-response exercise should always be performed as quickly off of the ground as possible.

OBJECTIVE *Enhances elastic-reactivity and improves take-offs in sprinting and jumping activities by using a "shock" methodology*

The depth jump is a "shock method" exercise and comes in the final phase of the training continuum. Therefore, progression into this drill is a must as well as progression within it, therefore you should start by dropping or "falling" off of a knee-high take-off surface. The key is to not initiate a rhythm of landing. This is to elicit the surprise of landing and subsequent take-off in as optimal an execution as possible. This applies to all sports because it employs leg strength, speed and quickness.

STARTING POSITION: Stand with your feet hip-width apart on a knee-high platform, the front halves of your feet just over the edge.

starting position

1 Drop from the platform and prepare for ground contact by bending your knees, keeping your elbows back and ankles locked.

2 The moment your feet touch the ground, take off immediately as high as you can. Eventually you can take off for distance. It is upon landing, not after, that the take-off is initiated.

OBJECTIVE *Emphasizes proper foot and ankle mechanics, positive shin angles, and hip projection—important skills for efficient sprinting and change of direction in field, court and track sports*

This is a low-impact bounding lead-in.

STARTING POSITION: Stand with your feet hip-width apart and your left foot forward, knees slightly bent and hips tall and forward.

starting position

1 Taking off with both legs, drive your right knee forward, pushing your hips outward and upward. The upper-body action is the same as in running.

2–3 Land on both feet with your ankles locked in a "toes up" position and drive forward with your left knee.

Continue this simultaneous landing of both feet and switching of the legs forward.

OBJECTIVE *Fosters good hip projection and back-leg push-off, emphasizes lead-leg mechanics and proper "pawing," or leg cycle mechanics*

This is a good rhythmic activity for early bound progressions and rehabilitation from knee and ankle injuries.

STARTING POSITION: Stand with your feet hip-width apart and your left leg forward.

starting position

1–2 Push off your right foot, keeping your ankle locked to emphasize a spring-loaded landing and take-off. Land on the left leg, keeping it in the lead. Stay tall, keeping your hips high with a cyclic recovery of the lead leg.

3–4 Continue this right-left, right-left, rhythm without crossing your legs. Imagine a barrier between your legs to keep them from crossing.

Switch the leg mechanics after a full set of repetitions.

OBJECTIVE *Works the striding muscles designed to reinforce sprinting and jumping mechanics with enhanced knee drive and hip extension.*

All skipping is performed by executing a step-hop pattern.

STARTING POSITION: Stand with your feet hip-width apart, knees slightly bent and hips tall and forward.

starting position

Fast Skipping: This is performed by maintaining close contact with the ground and eliminating air time. Maintaining as fast a rhythm as possible, drive the toe of your leading leg up and the knee forward and upward while keeping your heel up under your hips. Use an alternate (running) arm action.

Power Skipping: Obtain as much height as possible after each step by driving off your back leg. Drive the knee up hard and fast to help transfer the force from the support leg. Block with both arms for additional lift and hang-time.

OBJECTIVE *Enhances landing mechanics, forward hip projection, and the extension of the hip and knee necessary for improved acceleration in starting and stopping sports*

This drill helps progress towards bounding from one leg onto the other leg.

STARTING POSITION: Stand with your feet hip-width apart and your left leg forward.

starting position

1 Push your hips forward and outward from your left foot and leg. The right leg moves forward upon maximum hip extension and travel.

2–3 Land with a forward shin angle on the right foot and quickly extend from that position so that the hips remain in a forward position. This right-left-right-left sequence is essentially Bounding (page 132) without any knee drive.

OBJECTIVE *The prime exercise in specific development of explosive leg and hip power and enhance acceleration, sprints and jumps.*

STARTING POSITION: Stand with your feet hip-width apart, left leg forward.

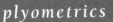

starting position

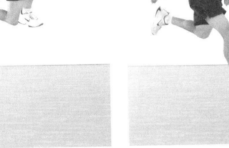

1 Push off with your back leg, driving that knee forward and upward in an attempt to gain as much height and distance as possible. Use the arms as you would in normal running, or do a double-arm blocking action.

2–3 Land and now drive with your right leg. Keep your ankle locked in dorsiflexion and the heel upward and forward in the driving leg for optimal hip projection.

4 Drive your left knee through and into the next bound for maximum distance with the least amount of time on the ground.

OBJECTIVE *Emphasizes use of the thigh and groin muscles to develop the ability to power-cut and change direction laterally in all field and court sports, skating, Nordic skiing and martial arts*

STARTING POSITION: Facing perpendicular to a destination that is to your right side, stand with your feet hip-width apart and hips and knees bent in a partial squat.

starting position

1 Lift to countermove with your right leg and push off with your left leg, driving your right knee to the right for distance.

2 Your right foot will land first, with your left foot following to balance out the landing.

Begin with single responses, then progress to rapid side-to-side multiple responses.

OBJECTIVE *Enhances elastic landings and top-speed (tall) posture*

A lead-in to proper tall posture single-leg hopping.

STARTING POSITION: Stand with your knees slightly bent in front of a series of 3–5 hurdles or cones spaced approximately three feet apart.

starting position

1

1–2 Countermove with your knees, hips and arms. Then take off, extending your hips upward as high as possible. Cycle both toes, knees and heels upward and over the hurdle. Maintain your posture and upright position by blocking with your arms.

Single-Response Hops: Hop over each cone, stick each landing with full foot contact, pause and then reset.

Multiple-Response Hops with Pause: Upon landing, pause for a brief moment, then perform the next hop without resetting the body. Progress to elastic multiple responses.

2

OBJECTIVE *Improves dynamic lateral change of direction*

Useful for agility work and as a test for lateral change of direction.

STARTING POSITION: With your knees slightly bent, stand directly to the side of two cones spaced 2–5 feet apart.

starting position

1–2 Take off sideways, hopping over both cones by tucking your knees and toes upward.

3–4 With minimal contact time, hop back over the cones.

Continue this back-and-forth sequence, blocking with the arms to aid in lift and posture.

OBJECTIVE *Enhances landing and take-off mechanics from ankle through hip.*

The beginning single-leg exercise helps train and/or rehabilitate sprinting and jumping off of one leg. In the early stages, this is best performed bare-footed.

STARTING POSITION: Stand tall with your left knee bent above hip level, the heel in front of your right knee. Make sure your ankle is lifted and locked with your toes up.

starting position

1–2 Bend then straighten your right leg to hop upward and forward, blocking with your arms.

3 Land completely on your right foot, with your shin and weight over your instep. Each landing and take-off should be felt high up in the glutes, not around the knee (indicating landing too much on the toes).

Repeat then switch sides.

VARIATION: You can also try landing on targets (plates, dots) to assist full-foot stabilized landings.

OBJECTIVE *Determines the ability to handle the posture, balance, stability and mobility of single-leg work*

This has prime value to all sprinting and single-leg jumping activities.

STARTING POSITION: Stand tall with your left knee bent above hip level, the heel in front of your right knee.

starting position

1 Bend your right knee slightly then jump up, sliding your right heel up and into your buttocks. Imagine standing with your back against a wall to emphasize that the heel should only come upward and not backward. Maintain posture and upright position by blocking with the arms.

2 Land full-footed with your ankle locked. Perform all of the repetitions with one leg then switch to the other.

starting position

OBJECTIVE *Mimics the body positions of top speed*

The ultimate drill for enhancing sprinting power, this drill can be used as an evaluation tool for speed and power. Begin with low hurdles or cones.

STARTING POSITION: Facing a series of 3 to 5 hurdles or cones, stand tall with your left knee bent above hip level, the heel in front of your right knee.

1–3 Countermove with your knees, hips and arms. Then take off, extending your hips upward as high as possible. Cycle the toes, knee and heel upward and over the hurdle. Maintain your posture and upright position by blocking with your arms.

First do *single responses*. When you are ready for *multiple responses*, attempt to keep the high swing leg position and match it with the hopping leg. Emphasis is on tall hips during landing and take-offs and cycling the heel up and over the hurdle or cone (approximately the same height of the opposite knee).

OBJECTIVE *Applies the power of single-leg hopping to diagonal change of directions.*

This drill is useful for anyone using speed cuts on a field or court (football, rugby, hockey, soccer, basketball, etc.).

STARTING POSITION: Facing a series of small cones or hurdles lined up in front of you, stand tall with your left foot to the left side of the first cone. Bend your right knee above hip level, keeping your heel in front of your left knee.

starting position

1 Take off with your left leg and hop upward and forward diagonally to the other side of the line of cones.

2–3 Land with full foot contact and immediately hop back over to the original side of the barriers.

Continue hopping diagonally forward down the line of cones.

starting position

OBJECTIVE *Applies the power of single-leg hopping to sideways change of directions.*

This drill is useful for anyone using power cuts on a field or court (football, rugby, hockey, soccer, racquet sports, basketball, etc.).

STARTING POSITION: Stand tall with your left foot next to a series of small cones or hurdles lined up to the left of you. Bend your right knee above hip level, keeping your heel in front of your left knee.

1 Take off with your left leg and hop over the cone to your left.

2–3 Land with full foot contact and continue hopping over each cone to your left with minimal contact time.

Pause at the end. Reset before you begin hopping on the left leg back to the right, then switch legs and repeat the course.

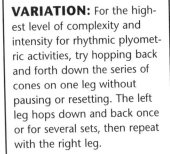

VARIATION: For the highest level of complexity and intensity for rhythmic plyometric activities, try hopping back and forth down the series of cones on one leg without pausing or resetting. The left leg hops down and back once or for several sets, then repeat with the right leg.

OBJECTIVE *Enhances hip and torso extension*

This exercise is very helpful for anyone coming out of crouched starting positions (sprinters, football/rugby linemen, wrestlers).

STARTING POSITION: With a 5- to 15-pound ball, kneel with the ball placed on the ground directly in front of the knees. Keep your chest out, your hips high and your back arched, with your shoulders positioned in front of the ball.

starting position

1 With your arms long and relaxed, shovel the ball from the ground in a line drive as far and fast as possible by quickly thrusting your hips and extending your trunk. Emphasize full extension of the hips and shoulder action, not arm action.

2 Land in a push-up position.

starting position

OBJECTIVE *Develops starting strength and overall power, improves coordination in starting, jumping, throwing, kicking, rowing, swimming, diving and sprinting*

This is similar to cleans and snatches, with the ability to release the implement.

STARTING POSITION: Stand with your feet slightly wider than hip-width apart in a semi-squat. With your arms long, hold a ball on the ground between your legs.

1 Extend up, keeping the ball close to your body by letting your elbows flare out...

2 ...then scoop the ball up so that both ball and body reach maximum heights in the air.

Allow the ball to drop to the ground and begin again.

OBJECTIVE *Works the torso muscles involved with body rotation, applicable in training for throwing and swinging (baseball, softball, tennis, hockey, etc.)*

This can also be done with a partner.

STARTING POSITION: Stand with a wall to your right. With your feet wider than hip-width apart and knees bent, cradle a 9- to 15-pound medicine ball against your body at about waist level.

starting position

1 Rapidly twist your torso to the left.

2 Abruptly twist back towards the right, releasing the ball explosively towards the wall. Concentrate on a rapid, reactive twisting action using your hips and shoulders.

OBJECTIVE *Improves hip extension, torso mobility and follow-through*

This progression of the scoop toss allows the ball to travel the greatest distance behind the body.

STARTING POSITION: Facing away from a wall a distance away, stand in a semi-squat with your feet wider than hip-width apart. With your arms extended, hold a ball below waist level.

starting position

1–2 With an initial countermove downward, scoop the ball and throw it upward and backward over and behind your head, attempting to elevate both your body and the ball for maximum distance. Distance backward is the primary emphasis.

Retrieve the ball and repeat.

OBJECTIVE *Improves the coordinated movements of flexion, extension and rotation*

This progression of scoop tossing and throwing involves more rotation that's very helpful for golf, track & field, gymnastics and martial arts.

STARTING POSITION: Place the ball on the ground outside your right foot. Bend at your waist and knees to grab the ball with both hands.

starting position

1 Scoop the ball upward and over your left shoulder, elevating both your body and the ball for maximum distance.

Retrieve the ball and repeat. Then switch sides, placing the ball to the outside of your left foot and throwing over your right shoulder.

OBJECTIVE *Improves overall power production with the overhead throwing motion as used in baseball, softball, football, soccer and javelin throwing.*

This can also be done with a partner.

STARTING POSITION: Facing a wall, kneel with your ankles relaxed and toes back. Keeping your torso tall and hips cocked forward, hold a 4- to 10-pound ball above and behind your head, keeping your arms relaxed and elbows slightly flexed.

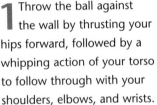

starting position

1 Throw the ball against the wall by thrusting your hips forward, followed by a whipping action of your torso to follow through with your shoulders, elbows, and wrists.

2 Bend at your hips as they go backward to finish the throw.

OBJECTIVE *Improves overall power production with the overhead throwing motion as used in baseball, softball, football, soccer and javelin throwing.*

This can also be done with a partner.

STARTING POSITION: Facing a wall, stand with your feet a little narrower than hip-width apart. Hold a 4- to 10-pound ball above and behind your head, keeping your arms relaxed and elbows slightly flexed.

starting position

1–2 Perform a line-drive pass toward the wall by bending your knees, thrusting your hips, whipping your torso and following through from shoulders to fingers, forceful enough to become airborne. Your hips will move backward to finish the follow-through.

OBJECTIVE *Improves overall power production with the overhead throwing motion as used in baseball, softball, football, soccer and javelin throwing*

This can also be done with a partner.

STARTING POSITION: Stand perpendicular to a wall with your feet hip-width apart. Hold a 4- to 10-pound ball above and behind your head, keeping your arms relaxed and elbows slightly flexed.

starting position

1 Step forward toward the wall with your left foot (if you're right-handed).

2 Immediately release the ball by thrusting your hips and whipping your torso while pushing off with your back foot, following through from shoulders to fingers.

OBJECTIVE *Emphasizes maximum push angles and timing*

This is a lead-in to the higher-impact pushing drills.

STARTING POSITION: Stand one giant step away from a wall and hold your arms slightly extended in front of you.

starting position

1 Lean and fall into the wall, "catching" yourself by bending your elbows and placing your hands, fingers pointing up, on the wall.

2 Immediately push yourself back to the starting position.

starting position

OBJECTIVE *Improves the power and elasticity in the upper torso needed in combative sports, racquet and bat sports, and rowing*

STARTING POSITION: Assume a push-up position by placing your hands on separate platforms with your arms extended. Your body should form a straight line from the top of your head to your heels. Maintain your posture throughout the exercise.

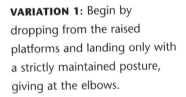

VARIATION 1: Begin by dropping from the raised platforms and landing only with a strictly maintained posture, giving at the elbows.

VARIATION 2: The next progression is to perform sets of a drop from the platforms and upon landing perform a full push-up while in contact with the ground.

VARIATION 3: This is followed by a drop and explosive push-up which results in the torso and arms being extended completely off of the ground before landing back on the ground.

VARIATION 4: The final progression is to drop and explosively push the torso and arms back up and onto the platforms with the least amount of ground contact time.

OBJECTIVE *Enhances hip and torso extension, helpful for coming out of crouched starting positions (sprinters, football/rugby linemen, wrestlers)*

This can also be done with a partner.

STARTING POSITION: Facing the wall, kneel with the 5- to 15-pound ball is held underneath the chest with your elbows in. Keep your chest out, your hips high and your back arched, with your shoulders positioned in front of the ball.

starting position

1 Keeping the elbows close to the ribs, push the ball in a line drive forward with the hips and shoulders, extending long and tall from the knees.

2 Land in push-up position and immediately regain the starting position, ready to catch the rebound.

OBJECTIVE *Improves the power and elasticity in the upper torso needed in combative sports, racquet and bat sports*

This can also be done with a partner.

STARTING POSITION: Stand facing a wall a distance away and hold a 7- to 15-pound medicine ball in front of you with arms relaxed.

starting position

1 Quickly push the ball towards the wall while performing a start or take-off in the same direction. Follow through with the initial steps of a sprint or move.

OBJECTIVE *Both stances improve the ability to project the hips from a good set position by pushing off with both feet and eliminating false stepping. In addition, the squared stance maintains squared hips during projection, while the staggered stance inhibits false stepping to the back and side.*

START SQUARED STEP: Stand with your feet slightly narrower than hip-width apart, keeping your toes aligned straight across from one another as if to jump for height or distance.

START STAGGERED STEP: Stand with your feet slightly narrower than hip-width apart, keeping the toes of one foot aligned straight across with the heel of the other.

1. Set your hips high and your back flat, creating a straight angle from the hips forward. Shoulders are in front, with knees over insteps (positive shin angle) as if to jump.

2. Cock the elbow opposite of the eventual lead knee backward, and the elbow on the same side of the predetermined lead knee forward.

3. Push into the ground with both feet simultaneously, shifting the knees further over the toes to project the hips forward.

Squared Step

Staggered Step

OBJECTIVE *Both stances improve the ability to "turn and run" by projecting the hips in lateral directions, pushing off with both feet, and eliminating false steps (back or sideways); they also improve cutting movements in field and court sports requiring rapid change of direction.*

STARTING POSITION: Facing perpendicular to your destination, stand with your feet slightly narrower than hip-width apart, keeping your toes aligned straight across from one another as if to jump for height or distance. Set your hips, keeping your knees balanced over your insteps and your back arched.

Open Step: Push off with both feet initially, driving your lead toe, knee, elbow and shoulder toward the destination. Your shoulders will dip to the desired direction. This requires a complete extension of the far-side leg and an opening of the hip as the near-side leg is led into the first step of acceleration.

Crossover Step: Push off with both feet initially, driving the leg and arm farthest from the destination toward the destination. Your shoulders will dip to the desired direction. This step requires extension and pivot of the near leg while the far leg drives across and turns the hips towards the destination.

Open Step

Crossover Step

OBJECTIVE *The drop step improves the ability to project the hips in backward directions by pushing off with both feet; it improves cutting movements in field and court sports requiring great agility. The pivot step improves the ability to turn and run by utilizing a rotation around a pivot foot; it improves some cutting movements in field and court sports requiring this type of agility. Both eliminate false steps (forwards or sideways).*

STARTING POSITION: With your back to your destination, stand with your feet slightly narrower than hip-width apart, keeping your toes aligned straight across from one another as if to jump for height or distance. Set your hips, keeping your knees balanced over your insteps and your back arched.

Drop Step: Push off with both feet initially, then drop the foot closest to the side of the turn backward and drive it to the desired destination. The leg farthest from the side of the turn is pivoted and pushes the hip to complete extension. It is important to keep your hips down until the drop is completed. Imagine being under a low ceiling to complete the turn.

Pivot Step: Push off with both feet initially, then cross over the foot farthest from the side of the turn to the desired destination. Pivot the trail foot and finish extending the leg to project the hips in the target direction. Your shoulders will dip to the desired direction.

The pivot step requires extension and pivot of the leg and foot nearest the side of the turn, while the far leg drives across and turns the hips toward the destination. It is important to keep your hips down until the pivot is completed.

Drop Step

Pivot Step

OBJECTIVE *Balanced start drills improve all of the previous forward, lateral and backward start abilities by taking away the ability to push off with both feet; by forcing you to set your hips with an arched-back position in order to maintain a balanced and "start-able" posture; and by revealing the need for the back or trail leg to be driven forward then actively pushed down and back into the ground, eliminating overstriding on the first step. In addition, they improve cutting movements in field and court sports requiring great agility.*

STARTING POSITION: Stand with your feet slightly narrower than hip-width apart, keeping the toes of one foot aligned straight across with the heel of the other. Keep your hips tall and your back arched. Bend one knee to bring that heel up under the same-side hip, approximately knee level.

1. Slightly bend your standing knee; draw your same-side elbow back. Push off with that leg and drive the raised knee in the desired destination. The arm opposite of the swinging knee should thrust forward at the same time.

2. Actively and aggressively push the foot back and down into the ground. Make sure you are balanced and stable on the driving (push-off) leg, that your torso is cocked and set for directional take-off, and that your hips are projected rather than dropped.

Note: The same balanced position can be applied to lateral and backward start movements. Adjust the position(s) of the swing leg and lead arm to accommodate for the angle of the lead step.

Forward Balanced Start

Lateral Balanced Start

OBJECTIVE *Loading or adding resistance to starting movements are helpful in developing both the power and technique required in push mechanics. Resistive loads can be in many forms: soft surfaces such as sand, gradual inclines like overpass ramps and moderate hills, or devices to load and emphasize hip projection such as straps held by a partner.*

GUIDELINES

- Place resistance at or on the hip bones.
- Athlete should control posture and balance rather than relying on the load.
- Remember to push with both feet and drive the necessary limb for proper hip projection.
- Make sure resistance is either constant or released upon push-off/transition to acceleration.

"a" walk / "a" skip / "a" run

OBJECTIVE *This is a necessity for every running sport. It improves acceleration, or push mechanics, and trains the body to project the hips and improve effective stride length.*

STARTING POSITION: Utilize any of the starting positions previously described (pages 153–57). It is best to progress through the starting positions in the same format as they have been listed.

1 As you step forward, pump your elbows backward in coordination with knee drive. Emphasize keeping your toe up and knee up in preparation for aggressive and active pushing of the foot back into the ground underneath the hip. Try to create maximum distance between the driving knee and the pushing knee. The toe is up to assure locked ankle landings and the shin is at a positive angle for pushing the hips forward.

2 The heel of the swinging leg should be in front of the pushing leg, not behind.

starting position

1

2

Basic Movement

PROGRESSION

- **Perform at walking tempo first.** Exaggerate the mechanics of tilting your hips forward and pushing back into the ground with your planting leg and foot.

- **Increase to skipping tempo.** Emphasize the extension of the pushing or supporting leg while driving the knee of the swing leg far apart from the support knee. Keep your hips tall and forward. A common mistake of the "A" skip is to "sit" or leave the hips behind, and/or allow the heel of the lead leg to swing backward, negating the proper drive of that knee.

- **Increase to running tempo.** Incorporating the Slide Kick (page 137) is a combination of the knee-drive and butt-kick actions: Imagine standing against a wall and trying to bring your heel up to your butt. Your foot/heel would have to "slide" up the wall in order to engage your butt. Emphasize explosive take-offs and pulling the knee upward and the heel forward and upward, not backward. This is a good way to work the "A" series at run tempo without fully sprinting.

starting position

Slide Kick Movement

OBJECTIVE *A necessity for every running sport. Improves hip projection and effective stride length, improves acceleration or push mechanics, maintains proper acceleration posture and active push against the ground.*

STARTING POSITION: Place your hands against a wall at shoulder level and push against the wall as if to hold it from falling on you.

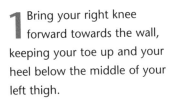

starting position

1 Bring your right knee forward towards the wall, keeping your toe up and your heel below the middle of your left thigh.

2 Without losing tension against the wall, quickly switch your legs so that your right leg is now back. This repetitive switch and hold against the wall will give you a better feel of the posture, foot placement and movement at the hip (rather than the knee) that is necessary for good acceleration.

OBJECTIVE *The thigh re-acceleration, or "B," drill is initiated with the toe and heel being lifted upward in preparation for the ground recovery. This is a necessity in athletes reaching high or top speed in competitive movements, and trains the components of high-speed running without voluminous amounts of maximum sprints.*

STARTING POSITION: Begin by standing with your hips tall and high off of the ground.

1 Lean forward and bend your right knee to lift the heel upward and slightly forward, up through and above your left knee.

2 Immediately re-accelerate your right thigh downward, pulling it backward underneath your right hip in a "pawing" motion. Make sure to keep your toes up.

starting position

PROGRESSION

- **Perform at walking tempo first.** Emphasize tall hips with the heels of your back (support) foot barely on the ground, the heel and toe of your front (swing) leg pulled straight up and cycled over your support knee.

- **Increase to skipping tempo.** Emphasize the rate of movement rather than distance covered. An original design of this drill was to be able to perform three re-acceleration strides per meter (approximately 2 yards). Keep your hips tall and forward.

- **Increase to running tempo** by using the cadence and fast leg series.

OBJECTIVE *This is an effort to employ a quick, light-footed rhythm to sprinting without reaching high levels of sprint intensity. It's helpful for any athlete who makes transitions to high speed such as soccer, field hockey, lacrosse, football backs and receivers, rugby, and track & field.*

STARTING POSITION: Begin with the same lean-fall-run positions from the B series described on page 161.

starting position

1 Start by running forward with short, light and quick strides (some refer to this as straight-leg bounding, others stiff-knee striding).

2–3 The right leg is continuous in its cyclic sprinting motion, with the right heel coming up to the butt, forward and around to touch down underneath the body again. The semi-stiff left leg is just keeping a quick supportive rhythm without the strides of a large cycling motion. The cadence can continue until you've switched to the other leg, or a series of combinations can be employed.

OBJECTIVE *Decreases speed, puts the body in position to move into another direction properly, and avoids unnecessary stress on the body*

Useful for all sports whether or not direction change is a factor.

STARTING POSITION: Accelerate to a moderately high speed for 5 to 15 yards.

starting position

1

2

1–2 Begin the deceleration process by bending your knees and dropping your hips. Keep your shoulders high and your chest spread. Your feet should land in full contact with the ground and stay beneath your hips.

Repeat this accelerate/decelerate process down the field in the following progression:

- Start barefoot in the beginning, to assure foot placement and mechanics.
- Increase the acceleration distance and decrease the distance in which to decelerate (e.g., accelerate 5 yards, decelerate in 15, then accelerate 10, decelerate in 10).
- Add a cut or break (direction change) to the deceleration.

agility training
sway drill

OBJECTIVE *Improves posture, balance, stability and power over the planted foot, enhances the cut mechanics used in sports involving change of direction*

STARTING POSITION: Stand with your feet hip-width apart between two cones placed approximately 2.5 yards apart. Keeping your chest high and your feet in full contact with the ground, lower your hips in order to be able to touch the cones with your hands.

1 Shift your hips sideways over one foot and touch the cone on that side.

2 Shift your hips to the other side to touch that cone.

PROGRESSION

- **Wide Sway:** Widen each cone out the length of your foot. Widen the stance and shift to touch.

- **Step and Sway:** Widen the cones another foot length. Return to hip-width stance, and then step sideways, shifting your hip out over the foot, and touch.

- **Pivot Forwards:** Widen the cones another foot length. Keep one foot planted in the middle and pivot around in a forward direction, touching each cone with the hand opposite the pivoting foot. Switch feet to pivot on the other foot and touch with the other hand.

- **Pivot Backwards:** Same as #3 only pivot backwards.

- **2-Step Crossover:** Widen the cones another foot length. This should put them approximately 5 yards apart. Step your right foot over and touch the right cone with your right hand, shifting your hip over your right foot to do so. Immediately push off your right leg, crossing over so that your left foot and hand are able to touch the left cone. Push off back and forth, taking only two steps in each direction change.

starting position

Wide Sway Drill

Step and Sway

Pivot Forwards

2-Step Crossover

OBJECTIVE *Promotes direction change without loss of speed, enhances the ability to handle small corners and lesser angles without drastic changes in posture*

This is useful for all field and court sports.

STARTING POSITION: Set up a slalom course by laying out cones, barrels or hoops in 5- to 10-yard increments, spaced apart at approximately 45-degree angles.

starting position

1

CONE DIAGRAM
start

1 Keeping your posture tall, accelerate into the course and continue to maintain speed or even pick up speed as you weave around the course. Make cuts by rolling off the inside foot. This is similar to a sprinter on the curve.

VARIATIONS: This can be run quickly in large circles or figure eights to work on the shifting of the hips and pivoting turns.

OBJECTIVE *Promotes efficient direction change, enhances the ability to handle sharp corners and large angles by quickly decelerating and re-accelerating*

This is useful for all field and court sports.

STARTING POSITION: Stand over a line situated between two lines that are 10 yards apart.

starting position

1

1 Sprint to the right for the 5 yards or until you're able to plant your right foot and touch the line with your right hand.

2

2–3 Immediately turn and sprint back the full 10 yards or until your left hand can touch the other line.

Continue sprinting back and forth.

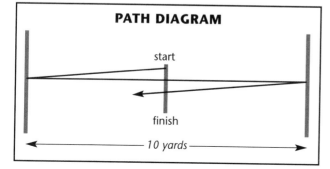

PATH DIAGRAM

start

finish

10 yards

3

starting position

OBJECTIVE *Promotes efficient direction change, enhances the ability to handle sharp corners and large angles by quickly decelerating and re-accelerating*

This is useful for all field and court sports.

STARTING POSITION: Set up a slalom course by laying out cones, barrels or bags at 5- to 10-yard increments and spaced apart anywhere from 90- to 180-degree angles.

1

1–3 Accelerate into the slalom course and perform the sit, dip and drive deceleration and re- acceleration (see Sit Drill on page 163) through the course. The cuts should be made by planting the outside foot and driving the inside knee in the direction of the next barrier.

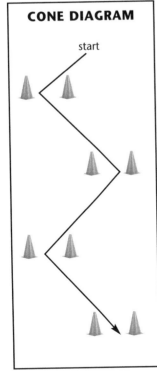

CONE DIAGRAM

start

2

3

OBJECTIVE *To use both speed cuts and power cuts in a measurable drill. This enhances the ability to handle sharp corners and different angles*

STARTING POSITION: Place cones in an "L" formation 5 yards apart. Stand at one corner.

1 Sprint and touch the line of the first corner.

2 Sprint back to the starting line.

3 Sprint back up and around the first corner, in and around the second corner (other end), and back around the first corner to the finish line.

USE THE FOLLOWING TECHNIQUE:
1. Power cut the hard angles.
2. Speed cut the soft angles.

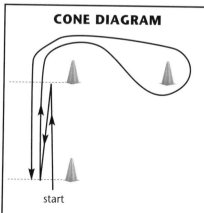

CONE DIAGRAM

start

OBJECTIVE *Utilizes both speed and power cuts in a reactionary exercise*

This drill basically has you racing from one end of the course to the other based upon the direction given once you are at speed. An excellent drill for any and all field and court sports.

This is a reactionary drill, which is the true key to agility training. Without a signal of some sort, either human or mechanical (which can be quite expensive) it isn't as reactionary, and would be the same as the aforementioned drills.

STARTING POSITION: Assemble a course with a start and finish lines. Place cones at angles to the outside of midline of the course (see diagram). A direction caller or signaler is placed near the finish line. At his/her command the athlete(s) sprint on a direct line towards the finish line. Before they reach the first break point the signaler has the option of giving them a direction. Whichever direction they give, the athlete(s) should be able to speed cut off of this break to the next cone then perform a power cut on to the finish line. If the signaler gives no direction it is a straight sprint to the finish line.

VARIATIONS

- Lengthen the course and add more outside cones for a 1-speed cut, 2-power cut situation.
- Have the signaler be at the start and the athlete(s) move backwards into the course. Upon the signal, react in a variety of directions and possible finish lines.

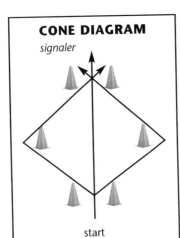

CONE DIAGRAM

signaler

start

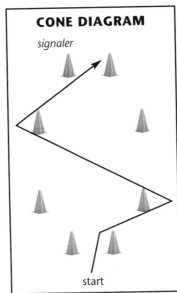

CONE DIAGRAM

signaler

start

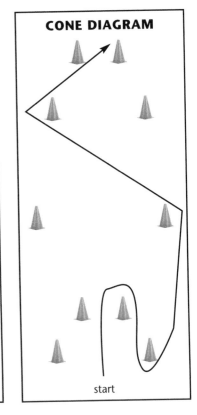

CONE DIAGRAM

start

starting position

index

references

Bompa, T. 1983. *Theory and Methodology of Training: The Key to Athletic Performance*. Dubuque, IA: Kendall/Hunt Publishing Company.

Bosch, F., and R. Klomp. 2001. *Running, Biomechanics and Exercise Physiology Applied in Practice*. London: Elsevier Churchill Livingstone.

Boyle M. 2004. *Functional Training for Sports*. Champaign, IL: Human Kinetics.

Dick, F. 1984. *Training Theory*, 2nd ed. London: British Amateur Athletic Board.

Gambetta, V. 2002. *Gambetta Method: A Common Sense Guide to Functional Training for Athletic Performance*, 2nd ed. Sarasota, FL: Gambetta Sports Training Systems.

Kent, M. 1998. *The Oxford Dictionary of Sports Science and Medicine*, 2nd ed. Oxford, England: Oxford University Press.

Mach, G. 1980. *Sprints and Hurdles*. Ontario, Canada: Canadian Track and Field Association.

Seagrave, L., and K. O'Donnell. *Speed Dynamics*. Euclid, OH. Video.

Starr, B. 2003. *The Strongest Shall Survive*, revised 1st ed. Aberdeen, MD: Fitness Consultants and Supply.

about the author

JAMES C. RADCLIFFE, the head strength and conditioning coach at the University of Oregon in Eugene, is a member of the National Strength and Conditioning Association as well as the U.S.A. Track & Field Association. He has coached at countless events, including the U.S. Olympic Track & Field Trials, the NCAA Basketball Championships, the Holiday Bowl and the Rose Bowl. A certified United States Weightlifting Federation level I coach, he has served as weightlifting official at the Goodwill Games. Radcliffe is the author of *Plyometrics, Explosive Power Training, Encyclopedia of Sports Medicine & Exercise Physiology* and *High-Powered Plyometrics*. His work has also appeared in publications such as *NSCA Performance Training Journal, Outdoor Magazine, National Strength & Conditioning Journal* and *Journal of Sport Rehabilitation*.

acknowledgments

First and foremost acknowledgment goes to Nick Denton-Brown of Ulysses Press for approaching me with the idea for this book. Thanks to Lily Chou for being a wonderful and dynamic editor, and Andy Mogg for his photographs. I also thank Mike Bellotti, the University of Oregon head football coach, for telling me I should do the project; and other Oregon Athletic Department members for their help with this process. Bill Moos has been a wonderful athletic director to work for and with. Thank you Gary Gray, Dave Williford, Oscar Palmquist and Jack Liu—I appreciate their professional help with photos and legal information. Much appreciation goes out to Vern Gambetta for his insight, enthusiasm, friendship and, above all, thirst for knowledge. Great help in the study of many of the concepts in this book has come from two wonderful researchers: Louis Osternig and V. Pat Lombardi. Many years of gratitude go out to my coaching colleagues Geoff Ginther, Jeremy Pick and Tom Hirtz, passionate coaches, fine teachers and good friends. I would also be remiss not to thank each and every coach and athlete who has come through the University of Oregon athletic department in my time—I have learned something from all of them.

Above all, I must acknowledge my family: Clay Erro, who for all intents and purposes is my brother, mentor and constant coaching inspiration; my nephews and godsons, my consummate training partners; my parents Bill and Helen, absolutely the finest people I know; and my wife Janice, the perfect teacher, researcher, professor, travel companion and best friend.